Water Walkers

Confront mediocrity
& step into your destiny

By Rebecca L. Bramblet

Water Walkers: Confront Mediocrity and Step into Your Destiny

Table of Contents

Endorsements

Rebecca is a living testimony that when the Holy Spirit is your constant trust and helper, you can defy the odds and have it all. "The process is where the magic happens. It's in the middle of the mess that you discover what you are made of."

It has been our joy to watch Rebecca and her family hold firm to the promise.

If you live it, you can give it. Her story is an anointed equipper's manual for your life transformation.

-Mahesh & Bonnie Chavda, All Nations Church,
Chavda Ministries International, Fort Mill, SC

This is a book that will fill you with courage!! Rebecca takes you on a journey into the heart of the Father...and you find out He is better than you think. Get ready for an upgrade in beliefs. Get ready to discover your identity at a deeper level. Get ready to take a risk for the King!

-Jim Baker, Senior Pastor, Zion Christian Fellowship Founder, Wealth
with God and author of *How Heaven Invades Your Finances*

This book will inspire you to go after your God-given dreams and confront the daily challenges that discourage so many from taking the first step toward destiny. Water Walkers will activate your faith for more.

-William Wood, Associate Evangelist Global Awakening

Sometimes following the call of God requires a giant near-blind leap of faith into a foretold future. The first steps must be taken before there is a manifestation of the prophesied promise or a confirmation of the way forward. It is the testimony of those who have leapt before us that gives us the faith to leap ourselves--those like Abraham, Noah, Mary the mother of Jesus, and Peter whom Jesus called out on the water. In *Water Walkers*, Rebecca Bramblet writes the story and lessons of her own miraculous story. It will give you courage to step out on the water and leap forward in your faith.

-Dr. Kim Maas, International Speaker, Founder/CEO Kim Maas Ministries, Women of our Time, Ten35Productions Author of Prophetic Community: Gods Call for All to Minister in His Gifts (Chosen Books, 2019).

If you have ever wanted to step out of the ordinary into an extraordinary faith-filled spiritual life, this book is for you. It is filled with time-tested truths that will enable you to quickly overcome the most common barriers and walk into a life filled with miracles that demonstrate the love and power of God.

-Scott Stoll, M.D. Co-Founder Plantrician Project, Olympian, Best-Selling Author

Dedication

This book is dedicated to my Papa God. Thank You for giving me the courage to step out of the boat. Thank you for giving me the story. Thank you for loving me through my brokenness and setting my feet on solid ground, even though it is wet. Thank You for the wonderful talks we have and the visions You give me to see the world through Your eyes. I love how You see life. I love how You see people. When I grow up, I want to be just like You.

I also dedicate this book to my husband, Troy. You are my favorite. I can't imagine being on this journey with anyone else. I love your strength and integrity, your gentle, but strong leadership, your faithfulness and dedication, and your uncompromising love and humility. You are an amazing husband and daddy, and I am honored God put me in your life to color your world. You will forever be my rock and I will be your butterfly.

To my children: Ashley, Caleb, Shanna, Abby, Nathan, and Micah. Thank you for opening your lives to the adventure. I know in many ways you had no choice in the matter, but I promise you that our heavenly Father uses it all to prepare you for your destiny… and man, do you guys possess an amazing destiny. The full vision has not yet been realized, but it is coming soon and we know it will grow on in your lives and in the lives of your children. Through this journey we have all reached our Promised Land and He is worth it. He is so worth it. Your mom and dad love you so much and couldn't be prouder of the young people you have become. We are so excited to see your own journeys unfold and witness how much farther you will walk on the waters of this adventure we call life.

And lastly to my friends and family who journeyed with us and cheered us along, holding our heads above water when necessary. Your prayers, generosity, laughter, hospitality, and comfort will be rewarded in Heaven and the seeds that you have sown will reap a harvest. We are surrounded by the most amazing Kingdom tribe and I consider my friends and family to be the richest blessings I steward. This is not just our story. It is yours too. We are all a part of a grand story; one I know makes Papa so proud to read. I love you and thank you for living life by our side. You are all Water Walkers!

The Cover Design

The cover of this book is designed on purpose to reflect the journey of a Water Walker. Water Walkers are pioneers. When they step out of the boat of mediocrity and into the sea of destiny, the answer to their prayers for "more" is unknowingly a time in the wilderness. Every serious believer goes through a wilderness time. It is a dark, contradicting time, when all beliefs are challenged. It is a time of sifting, shaping, and purging, but also, strangely, a time of comfort. In the book of Hosea, God is constantly trying to woo Israel away from her adulterous habits. He doesn't want her to walk in curses and hardship. He longs to see her restored and living the vibrant life He called her to.

> *Therefore, behold, I will allure her, will bring her into the wilderness, and speak comfort to her. I will give her her vineyards from there, and the Valley of Achor as a door of hope; she shall sing there, as in the days of her youth, as in the day when she came up from the land of Egypt*

(Hosea 2:14-15).

God's heart is to lure us into the wilderness where He can strip away those chains that bind, so we can walk freely. This is the voice of a God that loves and tenderly cares for His own. He knows exactly what we need to prune from our lives so that our vineyards thrive with life.

Water Walkers forge paths for others to follow. The path before them is not paved and at times feels dark and lonely, exposed and vulnerable. Even so, the sky is the limit to explore instead of a boxed-in, preset path. What I love about the cover is that the person walking needs only to walk toward the light of Christ. Peter, when he walked toward Jesus, was able to walk on water. No matter how dark and vast the world around seems, the truth is that we are not walking alone. In reality, we are held within this vast universe of possibilities inside our Creator's big, strong hands.

Cover design by Ashley Bramblet (my daughter). You blew this project out of the water, sweetheart. I love working with you. You are so gifted! Thank you!

A special thank you goes out to Kelli Billing and Troy Bramblet for their editing help and tireless hours spent pouring over the same chapters over and over again to make it look just right. I appreciate all the funny notes that made me laugh. I also want to thank Christine O'Connell, Amanda Port, Larry Remaly, Joe Mancuso, and Margie Negri for your keen eyes on the first draft. Having a second and third pair of eyes, especially for those Scripture references, was so helpful. I am glad we no longer have an identity bear in our midst. You are all the best!

Testimonials

The twenty years of doing life with the Bramblet family has been an adventure! We are blessed to call them our dearest friends. They live life in the deep end and encourage you to join in. They have walked a life of radical faith with joy, perseverance, intentionality, and humility. Our life has been rich and we have grown in ways not possible except for Troy and Rebecca's Kingdom-minded impact. We love them dearly and are excited they are sharing their wisdom through this book. It was hard-won through taking risks and stepping out, often without seeing the road ahead. We are not the same people we were, and you won't be either, if you receive and apply the wisdom laid out in this book. Brace yourself; you're in for a wet, but life-changing ride!

Lee and Kelli Billing

In 2007, my life was radically transformed through the ministry of Troy and Rebecca Bramblet. They invited me into a relationship with their family, offering to disciple me as a spiritual daughter. They counseled me through prayer, taught me to discern spirits and atmospheres, and released me to serve in their Deliverance and Inner Healing Ministry. They both carry a strong teacher anointing and I was hungry to learn. If you are hungry and thirsty for more of God in your life, their resources will inspire and motivate you to go deeper in fellowship with the Holy Spirit. Their wisdom and love over the years have catapulted me to walk in greater maturity to equip the body of Christ. The Bramblets' journey of trust and obedience with the Lord has marked them as pioneers of faith. I am honored to call them family and cherish the gifts they carry and share. They have always held me accountable and have been instrumental in helping me persevere in my own journey with Holy Spirit. I am confident that their ministry will advance and challenge you to step out of your comfort zone and launch you into your destiny.

Pastor Rana Walmer, DJ Momma Productions LLC

Our friendship with Troy and Rebecca has spanned twenty years. Their tenacity and authenticity to live out God's Word has been the greatest influence in our lives as we have walked next to them in ministry as well as raising our families. Through our life's experiences, we have been able to trust in their wise counsel and steadfast friendship.

Rich and Tracy Quamme

I have known Troy and Rebecca for almost twenty years. Their impact on my life is almost beyond words as we have been through the good, the bad, the ugly, and the beautiful together. Through it all, the words that would best describe their lives is an "intentional pursuit of the deeper walk." Spiritual growth and maturity don't just happen: they are pursued. Join the pursuit.

Pastor Larry Remaly

I am so excited that Rebecca has formulated her wealth of knowledge and experiences and put into print this inspirational piece. I am sure that many will receive healing from this book and there will be a rippling effect, because when one life is restored, peripheral lives are impacted. I have worked with Rebecca in a healing ministry and have seen that she has a powerful gift of wisdom that allows her to weave together threads of information; to see beyond outward situations and into the heart of the matter. Like an artist, her eyes are always fixed upon the beauty within each person she encounters. And she has the love and patience to bring breakthrough victory over all obstacles, escorting people to step into the destiny that God has ordained for them. Rebecca and Troy have been a steady and strong force that has helped me stay on course when I struggled with fear in my parenting of a 12-year-old son. And when I walked through difficult relationships, they taught me that if I keep love first and follow God, I will have victory. They have a gift of seeing and bringing out hope and God's blessings in all situations. Being with them brings one to a higher plane of thinking and living. I love them and know they were created for such a time as this!

Barbara LaBrie, Head of Freedom Prayer
Ministry and Instructor at Abundant Life
Equipping Center

Troy and Rebecca were instrumental in helping me overcome a tsunami of rejection which was literally drowning and destroying me. I am truly thankful for all the years they labored prior to that day so that I could be set free. I am excited for the countless others who will be launched into their destinies through them. They are a blessing and a sure delight to me and to our entire family!!! I am grateful and proud to call them my Friends!!! Watch out world, the Water Walkers are rising up!!

Kristen Stoll

Troy and Rebecca Bramblet have the integrity, revelation, and anointing to help others step into their destiny. Our lives have been forever changed and impacted by their ministry. We cannot recommend them highly enough.

Dominick and Natalie Cifarelli

The Bramblets courageously walk into areas that others shy away from. They have been instrumental in walking beside us and helping us claim freedom in our lives. They have shared with us the secrets to freedom that allow us to walk out our destiny, release us from bondage, break inner vows and generational issues, and even discover things holding us back that we were completely unaware of...all these, through yielding to the power of the Holy Spirit - the only way to walk in freedom. Their ministry is a peace-filled experience of cleansing your soul.

Keith and Marcella Holmes

Troy and Rebecca's ministry has affected me and my family profoundly. Through their leadership I have seen my children mature spiritually and learn to love and value intimacy with God as they grew in their identities as children of The Most High. On a personal level, I have been taught spiritual tools to use in my marriage and everyday life. The Bramblets walk in integrity and love; anyone who encounters them will be truly blessed.

Pastor Barbara Colacchia,

The 40 Day Experiment Achieving Intimacy with God

I have known Rebecca and Troy Bramblet for over 10 years. The word that I believe that reflects their character is authenticity! They have a deep, authentic love relationship with our Lord Jesus and a deep, authentic relationship with others. I have also appreciated and admired their deep unwavering trust in our Lord as they walked with God through over five years of challenging difficulties and hardships. You can know the depth of a person's spirituality in the way they respond to adversity. Rebecca and Troy hear the voice of God with clarity and follow Him with radical obedience. I have enjoyed their friendship and fellowship over the years.

Rev. Christopher W. Hussey, Senior Pastor,

Abundant Life Community Church

You will be very surprised to meet such an amazing couple who walk in the supernatural like it's natural. I have known Troy and Rebecca for many years and am still amazed by their faith. They are the ones who walk on water and are living their life stepping out in RISK every day. The joy of the Lord is their strength and you will be challenged by their radical obedience. When Papa God says jump, they will, knowing that He will always catch them.

Rev. Nataly Galichansky, Pastor of Ministry Development

at Abundant Life Community Church

My wife and I knew there was more to experience in our encounter with God and we were very anxious to go deeper with Him. Enter Troy and Rebecca. Our lives became intertwined these past 4 years as we did ministry with Troy and we began to experience God at a whole new level. It has transformed our walk with God. They have inspired us to "step out of the boat" and be who God created us to be. They helped us discover our value, purpose and the amazing gifts we have to offer the world around us. A major factor in our ongoing transformation is the unique experience Troy and Rebecca shared with us concerning what we call their "six-year fast" ... their harrowing trek across the country in search of that deeper connection to God's heart. Rebecca and Troy sold out for a more intimate relationship with the Lord, and we are convinced that their sacrifice was worth the heartache. Their six-year fast was not just for their growth, but it was also meant for our growth as well. We graciously embraced their heartfelt (and hard-felt) pursuit of God and are so grateful. There is more, so much more. We knew this truth, and then we saw it in the lives of our dear friends, Troy and Rebecca.

Tom and Nancy Plummer

The Invitation

When you are faithful with what is in your hand,
God will give you what is in your heart.

~Sean Cannell, author and YouTube artist extraordinaire

To Reach Your Destiny You Must...
Step Out of the Boat

What is a Water Walker? A Water Walker is someone who desires freedom, significance, intimacy, meaning, and fulfillment and is hungry for more in every area of their life. Their biggest "fear" is living a half-lived life of mediocrity and not accomplishing what they were destined to achieve...not fulfilling their purpose, dreams, or destiny. They may have gained "success" in numerous areas, but find themselves asking, "Is this all there is? Is there more?" They have reached what they thought would satisfy, but they find that it is not enough. They are sensing a need for a greater adventure; to build something with their life that lasts. Water Walkers look to see possibilities and then structure their lives around bringing those possibilities into reality.

They are pioneers and leaders not interested in just survival, but existing to find the secrets to a thriving, abundant life. We have learned those secrets. Water Walkers are Kingdom builders who are not afraid to embrace the training in the wildernesses of life if it means reigning in the Promised Land. I ask you this question: Why do in forty years what you can do in forty days? The Israelites wandered in the wilderness for forty years and yet Jesus set the example and walked His wilderness successfully in forty days…then He stepped out of the wilderness in the power of the Holy Spirit.

Is walking on water only for the super-spiritual: the pastors, the missionaries? Is this something you have to be "called" to do, or can the secrets to walking on water actually be taught and practiced by anyone? Can *you* walk on water? What if *you* could learn to overcome the obstacles that prevent you from stepping out of the boat? What if *you* could grasp the keys that would allow you to keep walking on the water, right into your destiny? Did you know that you CANNOT reach your destiny while sitting in the boat? In fact, that boat can become a prison keeping you from your destiny. I don't want this for you. I hope that in these pages, I will be able to expose you to and lead you to overcome the five obstacles keeping you in the boat of mediocrity. Mediocrity is a prison, a slavery mentality. I want to help you build a framework for a new way of living the abundant life, the Kingdom life. I want to teach you the secrets to walking on the water instead of sinking into it. I want our amazing story to inspire you to take that first, big step out of the boat. And when your feet get wet, that pent-up cry of "FREEDOM" will reverberate across that entire body of water as you, a new water-walking-believer, head toward your destiny!

"...you CANNOT reach your destiny while sitting in the boat."

"Middle of the Rock"

Mediocre is a term that literally means, "middle of the rock." It was originally a rock-climbing term that was used to describe people who made it only half way up the mountain. For example, there is a mountain resort in the Swiss Alps that caters to groups of climbers that set out to conquer the mountain. They usually start out in groups, excited and committed, but when they reach the half-way point, and they enter the resort to rest, refuel, defrost, or enjoy a cup of hot chocolate, many lose their motivation and decide to settle for the comfort of the "middle of the rock." The elements are cold and their bodies fatigued. After reaching their comfortable spot, they become satisfied with how far they have come. What they are not prepared for is the emotions that surface after watching the return hikers from their group, hours later, descending with a sense of accomplishment and victory. They had gone all the way to the top. Those who remained behind realize achievement could have been theirs, but instead, they have exchanged excellence for mediocrity.

We are all prone to settle for comfort whether we climb mountains or not. God wants us to live the abundant life, but many are settling for just good enough. When I look at the possibilities purchased through the cross, I don't want to settle for good enough...not when my Savior gave it all. Romans 8:32 states, *"He who did not spare His own Son but gave Him up for us all, how will He not also with Him graciously give us all things."* We aren't more spiritual or humble when we only receive part of His sacrifice. It is rather insulting. If I gave up my son so that others could go free and live in blessing, I would want them to spend his death extravagantly and take hold of all he provided through his sacrifice. When I saw what Jesus had done from this perspective, I wanted nothing more than to honor His death by living a life of excellence to bring Him glory.

"I don't want to settle for good enough when my Savior gave it all."

There is More

This is our journey. Our story. Our legacy. This journey is written through my eyes and experiences. My word is "transformation." My husband's is "influence." Together, we hope to inspire you on your journey toward more. There is more. There is a whole world of truth to awaken to, but in order to receive it you have to be willing to rock the boat. For heaven's sake, rock the boat and then jump out, start walking on the water, and never look back. The world will tell you to keep it safe and conform. Many churches preach the same message, but I am here to tell you there is a movement of believers who are actually learning how to believe. They are believers who are discovering the difference between religion and Kingdom. I have a passion to see people restored to relationship with God, living the life they were created to live instead of the life they have settled into. My husband and I have led an inner healing ministry for the past twenty years and have seen many lives (including whole families) transformed. The church exists to equip believers and send them out to bring heaven to earth (Matthew 6:10). Not all churches preach the same Kingdom message. The message of the Kingdom is all about believing. Believers believe…period. In fact, that is what walking on water is all about…standing on His word. There is a dream worth discovering and a destiny worth pursuing. It's worth the risk to step out of the boat, silence the waves, and walk on water.

"Believers believe...period."

Peter Walks on Water

Walking on water is the exciting adventure of life: a life of faith and guided risks; a life of miracles and divine encounters; a life walking on water with Jesus. Read and be encouraged as this once ordinary family of eight stepped out of the boat in 2009 and has never looked back. Let's start by being reminded of the literal account of walking on water. I have always been fascinated with the biblical account of Peter stepping out of the boat in Matthew 14:22-33,

> Immediately Jesus made His disciples get into the boat and go before Him to the other side, while He sent the multitudes away. And when He had sent the multitudes away, He went up on the mountain by Himself to pray. Now when evening came, He was alone there. But the boat was now in the middle of the sea, tossed by the waves, for the wind was contrary. Now in the fourth watch of the night Jesus went to them, walking on the sea. And when the disciples saw Him walking on the sea, they were troubled, saying, "It is a ghost!" And they cried out for fear. But immediately Jesus spoke to them, saying, "Be of good cheer! It is I; do not be afraid." And Peter answered Him and said, **"Lord, if it is You, command me to come to You on the water. So He said, "Come."** And when Peter had come down out of the boat, he walked on the water to go to Jesus. But when he saw that the wind was boisterous, he was afraid; and beginning to sink he cried out, saying, "Lord, save me!" And immediately Jesus stretched out His hand and caught him, and said to him, "O you of little faith, why did you doubt?" And when they got into the boat, the wind ceased. Then those who were in the boat came and worshiped Him, saying, "Truly You are the Son of God."

The truth is, there are waves we encounter in this life. How we encounter them means everything. There are people who are still on the shore watching the boat from the sidelines. And then there are those still in the boat who don't even think to test the waters and pursue Jesus in the depths. What a crazy idea, especially in a storm. The nerve of Peter to get such an idea as to walk on water! But he did. Even though it only lasted for a bit, he did. He had a crazy idea that there was more to this walk with Jesus than just sitting in the boat. He acted on his inclination that if Jesus could walk on water, then so could he. Jesus loved Peter's faith. He just wanted to see more of it. It was only when Peter took his eyes off of Jesus and focused on the waves that he began to sink. Fear and unbelief rob many of their inheritance. How far could he have walked if his faith had not wavered and he had been completely grounded in trust and obedience, partnered with a little bit of compulsion?

The Man in the Arena

One of my favorite quotes by former President of the United States, Theodore Roosevelt, is titled, *The Man in the Arena*, and it speaks to the same theme:

> *It is not the critic who counts; not the man who points out how the strong man stumbles, or where the doer of deeds could have done them better. The credit belongs to the man who is actually in the arena, whose face is marred by dust and sweat and blood; who strives valiantly; who errs, who comes short again and again, because there is no effort without error and shortcoming; but who does actually strive to do the deeds; who knows great enthusiasms, the great devotions; who spends himself in a worthy cause; who at*

the best knows in the end the triumph of high achievement, and who at the worst, if he fails, at least fails while daring greatly, so that his place shall never be with those cold and timid souls who neither know victory nor defeat.

It takes guts to enter the arena. It takes guts to step out of the boat. Many people are tired of fluff and mediocrity. They are tired of being inspired only to find out they don't know how to sustain it. They want more than the motivation and upsides that come from a constant cycle. They are hungry for freedom and want the tools so they can start building lives with meaning, passion, and purpose; lives that are free of guilt, disappointment, and regrets. They want to own their lives instead of being victims of society or slaves to their lusts and passions. They don't want to just be part of the masses: a number, invisible and alone. We were created for more. We were created for an abundant life. We were created to walk on water.

People may be tired of mediocrity, but very few are willing to risk and take the steps to be a part of the 2% of those who are hungry for more and are willing to risk comfort in order to attain it. Do you feel deep down inside that you are living a half-lived life? What this world offers is but a shadow of what is to come, as we were meant to live the abundant life in this world not just the next. Through a living, vibrant relationship with Father God, His precious Son Jesus, and the empowering presence of His Holy Spirit, I hope to demonstrate how you can walk on water. I want to show you that taking a leap of faith and risking all you know for all He knows is worth it.

Which One are You?

I carry a burden for three groups of people specifically: the person in the pew who wonders if there is more, the disillusioned Christian who has left the church looking for answers elsewhere, and the one who doesn't know God, but is curious and searching for truth. Which one are you?

Are you in the pew wondering if church is really relevant to life? Sometimes it feels like the church is twenty years behind the times and too impotent to deal with the issues that plague your life. To some, church has become a social club that looks no different from the world outside its doors--modeling for a lost world an empty religion of man-made "churchianity," as a friend of mine so eloquently puts it. Unfortunately, divorce statistics are just as high in the church as out, sickness and poverty abound amongst believers, and the pews are filled with broken families and enslaved people without answers. They need the power to change and the truth to heal, but don't know where to find it. In a culture where there are no absolutes, even many churches are buying into the lies and following, instead of leading culture into the way of truth, blessing, and true prosperity. Many churches have become an institution or a building we attend on Sundays instead of a living, vibrant bride. There has to be more. Does God have answers? You may have grown up in the church, and know all there is to know about religion, but do you really know God...and does He know you?

Are you the one who has left the church? Have you been disillusioned by a "hypocrite" who wears a mask on Sundays, only to live an entirely different life behind closed doors? Be careful not to judge all Christians by the few. Truth is, there are hypocrites inside and outside of the church. Broken people are being led by broken people, trapped in religious principles unable to tap into the power they read about in the Bible. They have explained away this power due to a lack of experience and inability to find transformed lives around them, pointing the way to freedom. People are leaving the church in droves over an offense, some as silly as the color of carpet chosen. Love of God has, in many cases, been replaced by politics and a religious mindset, and servanthood has been replaced by "rights." When did servanthood become weakness? If you ask me, it takes more character to lay your life down for another than to stand up and bark out your rights. Have you left the church because you don't see "Christianity" lining up with what you see in Scripture, or were you pushed out because you just didn't fit in? Have you always felt like a square peg in a round hole? Have you thrown the baby out with the bathwater? Or maybe you left church because you are mad at God, not realizing that perhaps you have some false beliefs, or lies, that are keeping you from the One who could be your greatest comfort? Then there are those who desperately love God, but don't know how or where to grow in their faith. You may be wondering if there are any "believing" churches out there. It seems wherever you look, men and women of faith are falling. Friends, people everywhere are falling, not just in the church. Who do you trust and where do you go with all your questions?

Maybe you are the one who hasn't even taken the step to get into the boat. Maybe you are one of those watching from the shore. Maybe all you know of God is what you see through the media, hearsay, or other believers who may or may not be living a life of faith. If all there is to Christianity is floating in a boat in the middle of a lake, then what is the point of that? Your life on the shore is much more appealing. Maybe you are stuck in a rut wanting to know if what you are living is all there is to life. Is there more? If there is a God, does He know you and does He have any answers?

If you have a dream in your heart that you think about when no one is around, I want you to know, He knows what it is, and better yet… He most likely placed it there. I know Christians have sent mixed messages and maybe your visits to church have confused you even more. Know there is an exciting and purposeful journey waiting for you and many churches are teaching this full Kingdom message. I would love the opportunity to introduce you to my God; the God I met through the pages of Scripture. He is amazing. He wasn't always amazing in my eyes because I had wounded filters and lies that kept me bound. I didn't think I could be real with God. I know differently now, and I would be humbled if you would walk with me on this journey to freedom.

I encourage all of you to pull up a chair, pour yourself your beverage of choice, and take some time to let God speak to your heart through our stories and the wisdom we have learned over the years. Enter into the adventure with us, and watch our family of eight live through a wilderness journey of discovering truth, growing in trust, developing skills, changing mindsets, and preparing to reign in our Promised Land.

"You may have grown up in the church, and know all there is to know about religion, but do you really know God… and does He know you?"

Become a Water Walker

Transformation and influence. Those are our mission words whether they be manifested in our parenting, our marriage, how we decorate our home, apply our gifts around us, the traditions we do, the food we eat, or the thoughts we think. We want to impart to you all that we learned on our journey of faith and risk these past twenty-one years. We also want to save you valuable time, expense, and heartache by giving you the secrets we have discovered to overcoming many of life's common obstacles and lies, so that you too may embrace a life of freedom, peace and prosperity, joy and hope, faith and love. Most of all, we have learned that He is the destination on whatever journey we are on. We find our place in Him and then we walk this journey together in fullness. We are all on a journey. Is your journey the one He prepared for you before the foundations of the world…that exciting adventure that only those who walk on water experience? Are you still in the boat? Are you safe and comfortable, coasting through life, hoping for an eternity of bliss when this life is over? Know you were called to the abundant life, *now*. Believers have a powerful role this side of heaven, to bring the Kingdom of heaven to earth. How we live our lives here determines how we spend our lives for eternity. Or are you still watching from the shore? Step in the boat and don't be afraid to rock it, or even step out and taste the freedom of walking on water. For all of you who are reading, I want you to know there is a dream worth discovering and a destiny worth pursuing. It's worth the risk to step out of the boat, silence the waves, and become a Water Walker.

CHAPTER ONE

Little House in the Valley

When we deny our stories, they define us.
When we own our stories, we get to write the ending.

~Dr. Brené Brown

Have you ever stepped out of the boat and walked on water…or at least wanted to? Have you ever stepped out of the boat and sank? Or have you passed on too many of those risky steps because of fear, being left only to wonder what could have been? Our hunger for grasping our entire inherited destiny simply would not allow us to watch from the shore or be content in the boat. We knew there was more to this life and we wanted it. While enduring the mocking of those still in the boat, we stepped out, and almost drowned a few times, but eventually we learned to walk on the water. We now have six children: Ashley, Caleb, Shanna, Abby, Nathan, and Micah. We are learning how to help them each navigate their own water walking journeys. We do this mostly through training and by leading through example. We love to watch God transform lives with His truth, by the power of His Spirit. That is why our hearts' cry is to empower and equip you towards life *transformation* in all areas, help you discover your *destiny*, and build a thriving *legacy* for generations to come.

Our heart and burning passion can be found in Isaiah 61:1-4:

The Spirit of the Lord GOD is upon Me, Because the LORD has anointed Me to preach good tidings to the poor; He has sent Me to heal the brokenhearted, to proclaim liberty to the captives, and the opening of the prison to those who are bound; to proclaim the acceptable year of the LORD, and the day of vengeance of our God; To comfort all who mourn, to console those who mourn in Zion, to give them beauty for ashes, the oil of joy for mourning, the garment of praise for the spirit of heaviness; that they may be called trees of righteousness, the planting of the LORD, that He may be glorified. And they shall rebuild the old ruins, they shall raise up the former desolations, and they shall repair the ruined cities, the desolations of many generations.

Once Upon a Time...

To begin our transformational journey, I need to back up to 2009. This was when my husband Troy and I both decided to step out of the boat. We had three children at the time and one on the way. Troy was an associate pastor of adult ministries in a medium-sized church in the rolling hills of northern New Jersey. I have always been a homemaker, homeschooling our children and learning as I went. Our passion has always been to equip and influence people and lead them to the deeper life. As we learned truth, we naturally encouraged others to follow along. When we began our ministry back in 1999, we believed we would always be content to live in a parsonage and remain at one church until we retired. We believed poverty was somehow part of the package. Now, we were nowhere near actual poverty, but as a pastor's family, we were told we would always be poor, we would never fulfill our dreams, and it was up to the church to keep us humble. In a sense we were honored guests, but could only eat the crumbs that had fallen from the table.

In spite of those word curses, we loved our life. We had a comfortable setup in a beautiful, picturesque valley; a country setting surrounded by farmland dotted with old stone cottages and quiet streams. New York City was less than an hour away whenever we yearned for the occasional Broadway show, world-class eats of any kind imaginable, or just a jolt of the city vibe complete with the echoing sounds of rushing taxis honking against the backdrop of skyscrapers that towered to the heavens. A day in the city was always a treat, but there was nothing like coming home to the quiet country life, fresh air, and open space. There was no place like home. We were surrounded by great friends whom we built our lives around. Together we celebrated birthdays, holiday picnics, and annual celebrations and we even vacationed together on occasion. We were working hard to eliminate debt and pay down our mortgage. We had goals of financial freedom, better vacations, a big family, the whole package...although it was laced with a poverty spirit disguised as religious piety. We loved God and were pursuing Him with our whole hearts and crying out for more.

When we began our life together, marriage was not all it was cracked up to be. Nor was ministry for that matter. There were years of brokenness and disappointments, financial struggles, and learning what real love was all about. We both had our baggage, as most couples do, but we were never satisfied with mediocrity. We have always wanted more and somehow, through the brokenness, we began the climb toward inner healing. As we studied the Bible (and any other materials we could find of people who were seeking more, dead or alive) we realized even most secular books just repackaged biblical truths into palatable phrases so they could sell to a different market.

These books were rich in wisdom, and yet many Christians had banned them out of fear of being led astray. They had more faith in the devil deceiving them than in God leading them. Although self-help or success books are good and serve their purpose, the Bible is the greatest book ever written. It's a living story and is to be read like God is talking directly to you. It is His mouthpiece to our world. It's His story; His love letter. Our inheritance. It has more wisdom, success tips, how-tos and direction than all other books combined. It also has amazing characters, good and bad, some that are G-rated and some R-rated. In it are the words of life, the invitation to true and lasting freedom, and a revelation of the King of all kings: our Creator and Father God, and His life-giving, life-changing Holy Spirit. The Word is perfect and a foundation of absolute truth that never changes and is relevant for every generation. The book of Proverbs alone, written by the wisest man who ever lived (apart from Christ), is chock full of wisdom and truth.

"The Word is perfect and a foundation of absolute truth that never changes and is relevant for every generation."

As we delved deeper into the Word, we began to realize our lives did not look like those found in the Scriptures, so we searched for mentors who could lead us in our pursuit of the deeper life. We couldn't find any in our circles. Jesus said in John 14:12: *"greater things will you do and more,"* and yet we were not seeing even the "great" things. Jesus modeled freedom for the masses. He healed the sick, raised the dead, and cast out demons; completely transforming every life He encountered. He was radical, and we were learning that His words and His truth were transforming our lives and home. Holy Spirit had become the Mentor we sought and we shared all He taught us with those around us and watched as their lives too became transformed.

I had not grown up in a Christian home, although there was religious influence from other family members. My parents divorced when I was young. Troy grew up in the church, but had wasted many of his younger years running from God after his father died. We felt like we were starting from scratch. Our parenting journey began with fear as our mentor: fear of screwing up our children; fear of making mistakes; fear of not being equipped to give them what they needed. Truthfully, I feared my children ending up like me, broken and ill-equipped for success. There is such a weight of responsibility that comes with parenting, and it is not to be taken lightly, but it doesn't need to be led by fear. When all you have is the example of those around you, and you strive to conform rather than live to be transformed, it can feel like the blind leading the blind. I have not always been as confident as I am now. I wanted to conform like the best of them, but I have always had this little rebellious streak that questioned everything. It was God's way of helping me learn to break out of the pack.

As we began our journey, we brought others with us. Many filled the Sunday school classes and Saturday seminars Troy wrote and taught, with an insatiable hunger for the deeper life. I led Bible Studies on inner healing and took all who wanted to journey into the deeper life with me. My love for God's Word was growing and I was beginning to trust Him more and more, but I knew there were closets I didn't want Him to enter. They were too personal, too painful, to trust to a God I didn't really know. But I kept pursuing because I knew there had to be more than what I was experiencing.

Troy and I were different. I don't mean different from each other (although we couldn't be more opposite in personality, which is why we're so dynamic), but I knew we had a calling on our lives that most did not. We would soon find out it would take us out of our comfort zones and answer our deepest cry for more. We found as leaders, we either inspired those around us, or made people uncomfortable; not because we were unfriendly or judgmental, but because others became dissatisfied with themselves after encountering the lives of two people in complete surrender. Many around us, unaware there was more, were satisfied with Sunday Christianity. But we were on a journey to the heart of God and were not stopping until we had all that was made available to us through the cross and resurrection of Jesus. We were finding it and lives were changing. And then…things got messy.

Secret #1

Determine to step out of the boat

CHAPTER TWO

So, We Bought a Ticket

———————◦◦◦◦◦◦———————

'Tis better to have loved and lost than never to have loved at all.

~Alfred Lord Tennyson

Careful you must be when sensing the future. The fear of loss is a path to the dark side. Death is a natural part of life. Rejoice for those around you who transform into the force. Mourn them do not. Miss them do not. Attachment leads to jealousy. The shadow of greed that is. Train yourself to let go of everything you fear to lose.

~Yoda

Until you believe that it is God who causes you to prosper, you will run around like an orphan trying to make something happen.

~Pastor Jim Baker, Zion Christian Fellowship

To say things were messy is an understatement. I don't mean chaotic, I mean messy. Most of us like things to be controlled and predictable ...*certain*. He is certain, but the journey most certainly is not. I can understand why people don't want to choose "the more." We like our comforts and predictability, especially in our western world. When God takes the reins, you just partner with Him and hold on for the ride. We don't ride rollercoasters because we like that safe feeling. We ride them because it makes us feel alive. One of my favorite quotes is by John Eldredge in the book *Wild at Heart*, "The glory of God is man fully alive." What a picture. It begs the question, "Am I fully alive?"

"The glory of God is man fully alive."

Here's another quote by C.S. Lewis in *The Lion, The Witch, and the Wardrobe* where Lewis is describing Aslan, the lion, through the character of Mr. Beaver. Aslan is an analogy of Christ:

> *"Aslan is a lion-the Lion, the great Lion."*
> *"Ooh" said Susan. "I'd thought he was a man. Is he-quite safe? I shall feel rather nervous about meeting a lion"...*
> *"Safe?" said Mr. Beaver, "Who said anything about safe? 'Course he isn't safe. But he's good. He's the King, I tell you."*

God is always constant and good, but the journey of faith is unpredictable and to be taken one step at a time.

2 Chronicles 16:9 declares, *"For the eyes of the Lord run to and fro throughout the whole earth, to show Himself strong on behalf of those whose*

heart is loyal to Him." Our heavenly Father is a wealthy investor who is looking for managers and stewards who will know Him and invest His resources and His heart wisely. You just have to read Matthew 25:14-30 to see this. He is looking for ordinary, broken people, who are hungry for more, that He can do extraordinary things through.

We Said Yes

Troy and I wanted everything that God had for us. We prayed that our lives would look radical and that our hearts and minds would be fully His. We said "yes" to whatever He wanted. We prayed this for years as we went to the Word to define our lives and our decisions. We signed our names on a blank document. As we surrendered our lives, we began to see the miraculous happen through our hands. At the height of our ministry, when the miraculous began to manifest like in the Scriptures–things like deliverance, healings, speaking in tongues, prophecies, words of knowledge, etc.; instead of celebrating with our church family, we ended up losing our job. Troy was asked to leave because our vision for the ministry had changed and it wasn't in line with theirs anymore. The Spirit was messy and not all were on board with what came with the mess. And that is okay. We love our first church. We grew up there. We had invested ten years of our lives into our church family and they into us. They raised us up and were now sending us out, so to speak. We were sad that theology issues had to separate believers, but we needed to be obedient to the call. Troy could have remained silent and kept his job. But then he would have had to squelch what the Spirit was doing in and through him. He was respected as a leader and his integrity was without question. It was our theology that began to manifest and it was time to move on.

When Troy came home with the news that he had lost his job, I was in shock. I had thought Troy would eventually become the senior pastor and we would retire there. That was the logical progression of things. We immediately prayed and asked God what we were to do. I heard, "I want you to camp across country." What? Come again? This is not the time for camping. I was thinking I must still be in shock. My dad and step-mom offered for us to come stay with them in Oregon. As we prayed, we couldn't get the idea of camping out of our heads. How would we camp? What did that look like? We wanted to understand everything. We were still very much operating in our logical brain. You see, the journey we were about to take was a journey that would teach us many things, one of which was the importance of saying yes without understanding. We were not to have an opinion, at least not until our opinions were sanctified. We would need to learn to live from the Spirit, and not the flesh, if we were going to live the life we were asking for. Our answer was an absolute "yes." On this journey, we didn't realize that we would be shedding many things including our reputation, friends, and the respect of many family members. Had I known what was ahead before I started, I may never have taken the journey because I did not have the capacity or the character at the time to sustain it. It started out wonderful, like a honeymoon, but eventually the testing would come. But I am getting ahead of myself.

We knew through praying, that we were to buy a van and camper and take time to cross the country. The logical thing to do would be to send out resumes for positions as a senior pastor, but God was calling us to healing, family cohesion, and rest. He would also reveal to us what we needed to know one step at a time. Like Abraham, we were to go until God showed us where and when to stop.

"We said yes..."

Order a Ticket

As he was finishing up the last few weeks of his position, Troy's daily commute took him past a Catholic church advertising a raffle sale with a brand-new Cadillac out front. He heard God say, "order a ticket." He fought the voice for two weeks; reasoning God was not into gambling and that couldn't be from Him. I suggested to him it was probably God and he needed to listen. Then he had this brilliant idea that God must want us to buy a ticket so we would win the Cadillac and then sell it and buy the van and camper we needed. He "knew" what God was going to do. God was packaged nicely in a box with a big red bow. How much could a raffle ticket cost anyway, 20 bucks? So, he called to buy a ticket and they said it would be $100. He thanked them very much, hung up the phone, and totally wrote it off as his flesh talking. God immediately came back with, "So you will trust me for 20 bucks, but not $100?" Convicted, he went and bought a ticket, then proceeded to tell me I was to wait by the phone on the day they were going to call the winners. When the day arrived, there was no phone call. We did not win. Troy was angry. He was trusting God and felt He had led him to waste $100. He also questioned if he was hearing from God. It was a critical time and he had a family to support. He couldn't afford to be hearing God wrong. I asked him, "Did God tell you to buy a ticket or did God tell you that you would win the raffle?" The point was to obey even when we did not understand or things didn't turn out the way we thought they should. The point, I believe, was to step out and take a risk, buy a ticket, and trust God.

Salvation and an Inheritance

Ephesians 2:8,9 states, *"For by grace you have been saved through faith, and that not of yourselves; it is the gift of God, not of works, lest anyone should boast."* Salvation is a gift that must be received through faith. You are saved through faith, but you also walk by faith. I love this verse because it is so foundational to a truth that would test us. It doesn't just state that we are saved by God's grace. We have a part to play. He has provided the way for all to enter into this grace, but it is only through our belief and appropriating what He made available to us, that we enter in. We need to receive it through faith. We have been saved by grace through faith. Get this because it is really important. When we receive Christ's finished work on the cross, salvation is a done deal. Along with salvation, comes an inheritance that is beyond what we could ever imagine. John 10:10 promises that He has "…come that they may have life, and that they may have it more abundantly." We spend the remainder of our Christian walk learning what the abundant life entails and all that was exchanged on the cross. When lack comes knocking at our door, or things happen in our lives that we cannot explain, if we don't understand grace, then we step out of rest and into works, legalism, striving, and performance. He has provided for us everything we need and we don't have to add to what was already accomplished on the cross. Grace (unlimited supply and ability) is His part. Belief is our part.

Let me give you an example of what our inheritance is, as His children, to hit this point home. It's not just the free gift of salvation. As a child of the King, there is more. If I was the granddaughter of a multi-billionaire, and in his will, he left me and each of his grandchildren a billion dollars, that would be compared to the abundance of grace and provision available to us through

Jesus. This grace was provided before I was born or even a thought on the radar except for my grandfather who decided to leave his future generations an inheritance. I didn't arrive in this world believing I had to perform or work for my inheritance. It was already mine. I was born into it. I needed to believe I already possessed it and receive it. I would need to appropriate my faith, to his grace in my life, in order to receive my inheritance. I am not saying every Christian is meant to have a billion dollars. It's not about money. Rather, I am saying that the provision, according to the vision that God has given to each of us, is accessed through faith. This is a learning process.

So many Christians believe God is good and owns the cattle on a thousand hills (Psalm 50:10-12), but they step into works and performance in order to receive it. When someone offers you an incredible gift, you receive it with thanksgiving, you don't perform for it. When we are born-again, we step into an inheritance beyond anything we could imagine. Our lives will naturally respond in love and gratitude when we realize that nothing we do or don't do can add to His love for us or His desire to care for our needs. This truth would be tested severely. Our journey would bring to the surface the lies we believed deep down, in order to shed His light of truth and set us free. There is purpose to the pain of the trials we encounter.

"You are saved through faith, but you also walk by faith."

Expectancy vs. Expectation

Were we willing to step out of the boat? We were learning how to live by faith and not presumption…to walk with expectancy and not expectation. God was giving us baby steps. Because God had directed Troy to buy a ticket, he presumed that God would have us win the Cadillac…obviously. Instead, he needed to have faith and expectancy that God was working, He is good, and He can be trusted. Faith is an expectancy that God is up to something good. It focuses on what God is doing. Presumption focuses on what we have done and our expectation of what God should do in response. Presumption is not faith. It puts demands on God and boxes Him in. Faith is teachable and opens you up to dream bigger. **Faith is living in expectancy and not expectation.**

Order the Van, I'll Take Care of You

We had some money from the sale of our house, so we went looking for a van and camper. The camper we found cost about $27,000. It was big enough to live in with a family of six. I had just had Abby (#4). She was three months old when we left. Springing money for a van was a bit more difficult. There were no used vans for what we needed…anywhere. We had to look at brand new vans and they cost a pretty penny…$42,000 worth of pennies, actually. We told the dealer we would go home and pray about it. As we drove off the lot Troy heard God say, "Order the van, I'll take care of you." He turned to me and said, "You remember the voice that told me to buy the $100 raffle ticket? Well, now it is saying to order the $42,000 van." So, I answered, "Then we order the $42,000 van." It made no sense.

The van and camper would drain all of our savings for the trip out West. But we ordered both the van and camper anyway.

A few weeks later, Troy came home from work and said, "I think we have our confirmation that we are supposed to camp across country in a van and camper." He continued to relay the story that had transpired earlier that day. After Sunday school, a man approached him and confessed that he and his wife had been praying individually and heard God tell them that we would be camping across country and needed transportation as well as a camper. The man asked if we were planning on camping. Troy hesitated because he thought the guy would think we were nuts. Troy confirmed that we were (camping, not nuts), but that is all in the eyes of the beholder. The man responded so confidently that he and his wife needed to take a step of faith and buy us the van and camper. We would later find out that their own journey of faith led them to this point. They were broken and so desperate for God. His answer to them was to step out in faith and sacrifice and bless us. Their lives have never been the same. God has opened up the storehouses over them, trusting His stewards to invest His money wisely. In doing so, they proved they did not have a love of money, nor a fear of losing it. Money served them, and not the other way around.

Sowing Seeds of Trust

When you plant an apple seed, you expect to harvest apples. One seed produces a harvest. That is how the Kingdom works. Now, I want to make very clear what I am not saying. I am not saying we use God to get money. That would be totally backwards, as we use money to serve God. I am also not saying that the path to provision for our needs is through giving. Giving is a key to increase, but it is taught from pulpits everywhere that "if you have a need, sow a seed" and that is simply not the heart of the Father. There is a spiritual law of sowing and reaping, it is just not to be used to get your needs met. Otherwise, that would be fostering a theology based on works instead of the truth that God loves His children and He takes better care of them than the sparrows (Matthew 6:26). We sow, to demonstrate our faith in a Father is a never-ending source of provision. By sowing, we are reflecting the intimacy level we have with our Father. When we give, we reflect His abundant nature. Luke 6:38 demonstrates this principle, "*Give, and it will be given to you: good measure, pressed down, shaken together, and running over will be put into your bosom. For with the same measure that you use, it will be measured back to you.*" We should be so excited to give because, when we do, God moves, and we get to stand back and watch Him love on His children. When we give with resistance, it reveals the hold that money has on our hearts. I love Matthew 6:24 in the Passion Translation. "*How could you worship two gods at the same time? You will have to hate one and love the other, or be devoted to one and despise the other. You can't worship the true God while enslaved to the god of money!*" The area of giving reflects our trust and intimacy level with God like nothing else. God invites us to give for our own sake, because He knows the hold money can have on a heart. He desires us to be free of the love of money, so we can be about building the Kingdom. He wants to purify our motives so He can prosper us in life and set us free to give. **He doesn't want His people to wonder where money is going to come from, but rather to live in the wonder of His goodness.** His plan is to draw us deeper into intimacy with Him, where we can trust Him with all that flows through our lives. When we are faithful with the little things in life, like money, He will put us in charge of greater things. We have the privilege of partnering with God and giving of our time, money, and talents. Sowing these into good soil produces much fruit for the Kingdom. Remember, our heavenly Father is a wealthy investor looking for faithful people to steward His wealth. It is all His anyway. This couple faithfully sowed their money into good soil, and they reaped a harvest. Two days later he brought over a check for $70,000 and presented it to us with such delight. He was free and we had the confirmation and provision to go on our own journey. "Order the van, I will take care of you." God had told us that the church was not our provider. He was. We just had to trust Him. We said yes, and He was faithful.

"Order the van, I'll take care of you."

Basement Church

After Troy was fired (which we later reframed into 'being promoted'), we began meeting in our friends' basement on Friday evenings. We were just soaking in all that we were learning, going out and practicing what we read, and coming back to share our stories and experiences with our friends. This in turn encouraged us all to go out and do it all over again. It felt like the Upper Room every Friday. We worshipped, danced, prayed, read the Word, and the children would lay sprawled out on the floor with paint and canvas and transcribe through color what Holy Spirit had impressed upon their hearts. It was amazing how everything flowed and connected. We had a basement revival going on. God was imparting to us all our own visions, callings, and destinies. We would forever be knit together as we went out. Just like in the book of Acts. On those Friday "basement church" nights the "more" had descended and it was there for the taking.

One Friday we had a visitor from the West Coast, from Bethel Church in Redding, California, who had heard about our on-fire group while holding a conference at a local church in the area. They came to see what was going on in our little basement church and encourage us in our walk with the Holy Spirit. As we sat in a circle, people began to share their testimonies, one by one, about how they had either come to Christ or found freedom and courage to step into the deeper life. As we went around the room sharing, our visitor looked over at both Troy and me, and said in a tone so full of reverence and honor, "Do you hear the lives you have touched in this room? Everyone here has shared how your lives have impacted them and they will never be the same." I was undone. I felt as though my heart would burst. First, because I loved these people and every detail of their stories was etched in my heart forever, and second, because I was humbled at how God had used us so deeply when we had been so broken. All we did was say "yes" and He transformed our lives. As a result, we were given the privilege of pouring into others all we had learned. This was our tribe. And now we were saying goodbye or was it "farewell, until we meet again?" We didn't know. We were asked to stay and start our own church. We had a choice: start our own church or accept the invitation from God to go on an adventure. Neither choice was wrong and neither was right. We were free to choose. Troy didn't want to be divisive and cause problems for the church we had just left. But my heart was torn. I prayed and asked God what we should do. He wanted to teach me to make decisions confidently as a well-loved daughter and not out of fear of making the wrong decision.

"We were free to choose."

Sheik Dream

That night I had a dream. God would actually present an invitation for me to trust my own heart to decide which direction to pursue. I didn't know it then, but it was a dream that would become the starting point for the future vision God would be unpacking on our journey. He knew I needed to know what my heart truly wanted to do. In my dream, a sheik was coming to town. He was looking for a bride amongst the people. I was to journey home to my parents' house to prepare. They counseled me that I needed to stand out from among the rest and catch his gaze. Preparations had been made, beauty treatments administered, and the day came for the sheik to arrive. Thousands lined the streets of the city as his entourage broke through the crowd. Arms waved madly from the sidelines and the screams and cheers were deafening. As he made his way around the bend, I stepped out from the crowd into his path. I cupped his face in my hands and kissed him on the lips. He turned his gaze toward me and our eyes locked. Then a woman stepped out from behind me and began to tell me that now it was time for me to prepare my gown. I would need to travel to different places and gather six or seven different materials, one from each place. Then I would need to prepare my gown…or I could buy one already made for $19.99. Somehow, I knew that I was making a wedding dress, because the sheik had chosen his bride. Then she disappeared and I woke up.

Troy and I started our ministry in 1999. We could stay and start a ready-made church, but I knew my heart wanted the adventure. I knew that in the searching for materials, my gown would be much more precious and my love for the sheik would grow much deeper. I would be building a love between us that would answer the cry of my heart to know and be known. I also was aware that there was so much more to learn and grow in that we would eventually be able to pour into others. **I chose the adventure. I chose the "more."** Now we were both in and the adventure would begin.

Saying Goodbye

Our friends came to help us every day to transition us out of the house. We would be living in the camper in the side yard until moving day. We packed boxes and moved them out sorting them into piles. Piles to stay. Piles to go. Piles to give away. It hadn't felt real until this point. Everyone showed up to help, but no one wanted us to go. We were going on the adventure, but they were getting left behind and would somehow have to find a way to fill in the holes. They had lost their church, community, and friends, but they had each other and they had a new purpose.

That afternoon everyone was asking questions, firing at me left and right, and I was just trying to process and take it all in. While walking up the basement stairs, I carefully took down all the tiny, multi-colored, craft paper handprints stapled to the wall that I had collected from the children over the years. I was leaving a life I loved and my heart was broken. I had to keep going and yet I felt like I was in a daze, or a nightmare, that I couldn't seem to wake from. With all the continuous questions, it felt like the world was spinning and I could feel the tears well up and my chest tighten. I couldn't breathe. Grief had hit me all at once and knocked the wind right out of me. I felt a sudden surge of panic and yet I didn't know where to go. My friend Lee could see in my eyes what was happening. As a big brother, he grabbed me and held me to his chest. I cried heaving sobs and let it all out.

Transition is a bittersweet time. I didn't want to stuff my feelings. I needed to learn to process them with God. It was okay that I had these feelings. He gave us emotions so that we could experience the world around us, but they are not trustworthy enough to lead us. They give us clues as to what is going on inside so that we can discover truth. These moments become invitations to a conversation with your heavenly Father. He wants to hear it all and bring His perspective. I had grown up feeling I had to perform and fix myself before I came for help, until eventually, I didn't come for help at all. I learned to do it on my own. This journey would be an unraveling of my belief system and a rebuilding of my soul, so that I could find freedom and learn to live from rest. This is what every journey can become…an invitation.

One afternoon, just before we were taking off, I sprawled out on the grass gazing up at the clouds while praying. My children and I love watching cloud formations pass as we point out different animals, figures or anything else that jogs the imagination. It is fun to see what others discover and it becomes a wonderful time to just talk and giggle. Well, this time, it was just me and God. While praying and watching the clouds pass,

I looked up and noticed a perfect eagle formation in the clouds, with its wings outstretched and its head held high and confident. All of a sudden, the cloud stopped right above me. It was as if the heavens stopped just to deliver a message and envelop me in those wings of love. In my heart I heard Psalm 91 verses 1-4:

> *He who dwells in the secret place of the Most High Shall abide under the shadow of the Almighty. I will say of the Lord, "He is my refuge and my fortress; my God, in Him I will trust. Surely, He shall deliver you from the snare of the fowler and from the perilous pestilence. He shall cover you with His feathers, and under His wings you shall take refuge; His truth shall be your shield and buckler.*

We were under His wings. He would protect us.

We set off on October 3, 2009. We were driving away from all we knew, all that was normal. We would be towing our 34 ft house everywhere we went and we would have a new backyard every few days. How exciting. We had no idea where the road would take us. So many dream about the journey, but few ever take it. We had packed everything we owned into a friend's warehouse. We carried only what we thought we would need to head out west to stay with my family in Oregon. Our "tribe" all came out to see us off. The ones we built our lives around. In their faces were the memories of a life well-lived.

I will never forget the moment Ralph came to say goodbye. There was something so otherworldly about our exchange that day, that brought me such peace. I knew we were going to be okay. Ralph and his wife Mary Ellen were friends that were also family, and going over to their house for dinner was like coming home. Ralph and I didn't need words to communicate. We spoke with our hearts and sentences flowed in our eyes. He always called me to his side, as he carved me the special, fatty piece of roast "beast" at Christmastime, both of us smiling as if to say, "it's a beautiful thing." Ralph has an amazing testimony that brought him to our previous church. He was struggling to find God and decided to call out to Him in his pickup truck one night. Just then, an advertisement came on the radio announcing a men's small group Bible study on Wednesday nights. Since it happened to be Wednesday, he decided to head on over and give it a try. When he arrived, it was Troy and our friend Larry that welcomed him. He proceeded to tell them that he came because of the radio ad. They quickly corrected him, telling him that our church didn't have a radio ad for men's Bible study. I guess it was a divine appointment that needed to happen. Ralph just credits it to Radio WGOD.

That afternoon, as we were pulling out, all our tribe was there to see us off. Ralph stopped by to say one last goodbye. It was short and sweet. He cupped my face with his trembling hands and kissed me and said, "This isn't goodbye. I'll be seeing you," and he walked away without looking back, flinging his arm over his head in a goodbye gesture, as he walked toward his truck. People deal with grief in many ways. His was a grief of selling out and counting the cost. He had entered the game and played hard and came out on the other side, all the stronger because of it. We all had, and that is why the pain hurt so deeply. What would we encounter along the journey? What did our yes mean and what would be the consequences of signing that blank document? **There is a cost and sometimes the doubt is real and the adventure hurts. But even the pain brings with it a collateral beauty.**

Secret #2

Faith is living in expectancy, and not expectation.

Secret #3

When we sow financial seeds, we demonstrate our faith and intimacy level in a Father who is a never-ending source of provision.

CHAPTER THREE

Is the Camper Still on the Road?

When we go to Europe we pay with Euros. In heaven's economy...we use faith.

~Kelli Billing

We called this our "Freedom Tour," but in reality, it felt like anything but. We jokingly referred to our little home on wheels as our sanctification incubator. There were six of us crammed into a tiny space. The children ranged in ages from 0-8. There was nowhere to go, so if there were problems, and there were, they had to be dealt with immediately. I wrote a blog as we traveled across country. It was my way of processing and recording our memories, as well as staying connected to those traveling with us vicariously. One afternoon, the title for the day's blog, *Is the Camper Still on the Road?* came pouring out of Troy's lips as he was white knuckling the steering wheel down a steep canyon with no guard rails and nowhere to turn around. While on Hwy 219 in Maryland heading into West Virginia, the GPS directed us to make a turn. Because it was getting late, we chose the "shortest route." Before taking off, Troy had never towed anything besides a lawn cart before and only had a one-hour practice session from Papa Jac, a former truck driver and dear friend. We had fifty-three feet of vehicle we needed to navigate and once we turned, we were committed. The gravel road seemed to narrow and the guardrails soon disappeared and then there it was: the most amazing view I had ever seen, since the Grand Canyon when I was just a kid. You haven't lived until you've seen the Appalachian Mountains in the fall, while hanging over the edge of a cliff. Troy could have lived without it, but then again, I wasn't the one white knuckling it. I have never heard him pray so much, or be so grateful as he thanked God after every hairpin turn, of which there were many. We could watch on the GPS the turns in the road that were ahead. With each turn, Troy would take a deep breath and often exclaim out loud, "you have got to be kidding!" The road just wound down deeper and deeper, into the mountains where the real mountain people live. I'm talking outhouses and the whole shebang. It was beautiful and creepy at the same time.

"Is the camper still on the road?" pretty much summed up how we felt during most of our journey because we were pioneering a trail for which there was no visible path before us. We were unclear of the destination, but we were shedding many mindsets on this journey of healing, rest, and family cohesion. So, there we were wandering in "Outhouseville" in the pitch dark with cliffs all around, no cell service, a nearly empty gas tank, and now, bonus…the camper's lights were mysteriously not working. All we could see were the headlights in front and hear the "creak, creak, creak" of the camper following close behind us. It's such a picture of the walk of faith. Psalm 119:105 says, "Your word is a lamp to my feet and a light to my path." Sometimes He illuminates the whole path. Many times, we are only given enough light to see what is directly in front of us. But we can rest in the fact that He sees it all even if we can only see one step at a time. Remember Peter shouted out, "Lord, if it's really you, then have me join you on the water!" Jesus replies: "Come and join me." The only thing we knew is that we were not called out onto the water to just wander and sink. We were called out to walk toward Him, and eventually with Him. **Faith is simply seeing things from God's perspective and coming into agreement with Him.** And as long as our eyes remain on Him, we walk on the water and join Him in the depths. We walk toward Him and cling to His promises, but it may feel like we are lost in the dark with cliffs on either side, and the only thing we know to do is put one foot in front of the other and keep our eyes on Him.

On the journey, we all battle the same obstacles: fear, unbelief or limiting beliefs, the past and a bruised or wounded identity, legalism or a religious mindset, and a lack of character— including pride, greed and selfishness. These will just manifest in different ways. Your journey will be unique to you. We would love to help you navigate your journey, so you are not walking alone. The hardest part for us was that we felt so alone. We were stepping out into uncharted territory and those around us either looked at us like we had lost our minds, or thought we were really brave. The reactions of people along the way varied greatly. Many told us they wished they could take steps like us, but they just didn't know how. Others believed the opposite; that they could never step out in faith like we had.

"...you have got to be kidding."

Noah's Wife Cried...a lot

It would have been helpful to know the obstacles we would encounter and have someone to hold our hand when questions came up. We had to piece things together as we went forward. The characters in Scripture became our greatest friends. No longer were they stories of faceless men and women, but now they had emotions, dreams, and daily lives. I remember when we were in Texas and my husband's job was driving Yogi Bear around the campground for weekend visitors. I realized—Noah's wife, who doesn't even have a name in the Bible, must have cried... a lot. Her husband hears from God that rain is coming and will flood and wipe out the earth. What is rain? The earth had never even experienced rain before because they lived under a canopy and the earth was watered from the ground up. He was commissioned to build a large boat for those who wished to be saved. Oh, and another thing...God would send animals to him of every kind. Minor detail, but it would take about a hundred years to build this boat.

All of their friends disowned them. Nobody listened to them. I am sure she must have doubted that her husband heard right. I am sure it hurt deeply that they were mocked and alone. But Noah believed God. I have never read the story the same way since. Sometimes God delivers us from our problems, other times we are delivered through them and we ride above them in an ark. The point I am making is that when the characters in Scripture become real people, it gives you faith and hope to keep going. I am sure Noah's wife cried, but she kept going, supporting her husband, and was saved to start a whole new beginning in God's story. We don't always receive the vision though. Sometimes we are building for another generation. Many in the hall of faith in Hebrews 11 never saw their promises fulfilled. Still they all walked toward the Promised One and I know they would all say it was worth it. I wouldn't change anything on our journey, except to maybe have more hope, trust more, and believe more. But as far as the lessons we learned, what we gained far outweighs any momentary sadness.

Wallowing in Washington

Most of the time, Troy and I kept the faith, but if one of us was down, the other was usually there to encourage and offer strength. But one time, in particular, we both were down. Being new to this prophetic walk, we thought this was how it worked: you were given a word and then it was going to happen in a few days. We would wait and nothing would happen. We were told to go out to Oregon to rest and God would give us the vision for the next step. Troy had gone to college, seminary, applied for a position and started his first job as an associate pastor. That was how it worked for us in the past. This was like no other journey we had ever been on nor one we had ever seen before, except in Scripture. We tried to follow the characters in the Bible, but quickly realized even people in the Scriptures had their faults. Jesus alone, according to Hebrews 12:2, is *"the author and finisher of our faith."* All eyes must be on Him.

Feeling all alone and wandering, we were both discouraged. We decided to cheer ourselves up one weekend and shoot up to two of my bucket list destinations of Seattle and Leavenworth, Washington. Anyone else dream of ordering a fish from Pike Place Fish Market for the sole (get it? I'm so "punny") purpose of watching the fishmongers "throw" your purchase as part of their theatrical display for the tourists? Well I did. My dream was crushed when I found out one fish cost over a hundred bucks. Needless to say, we enjoyed the show anyway. I had wanted to visit Seattle ever since watching the movie *Sleepless in Seattle*. I had also heard Leavenworth was beautiful, like a Little Switzerland. Anyway, we had one of those RV state sticker decals on our camper and we couldn't come this far and skip Washington. Leavenworth was a town out of a storybook. It truly was one of my most favorite destinations in the whole country. We had the most amazing ice cream, walked the streets, perused quaint shops, visited the cutest little bookstore, toured flower gardens, and spent time with the locals at their farmers' market. This amazing little piece of heaven was surrounded by the tallest, snowcapped mountains, as if we had been transported to Switzerland itself. Our campsite rested alongside a roaring waterfall with spiked mountain cliffs. I would move there in a second. The food alone is amazing. You can't beat the Pacific Northwest for food and cultural pride, not to mention BEAUTY. We saw so many beautiful places on our journey, but in our "intentional" minds it wasn't supposed to be a giant vacation. It felt like we were wasting time, even if we were wasting it in the most beautiful places imaginable. God is in the journey. He is all about living from rest and He knew that is what we needed.

Back at camp, we both lay on the bed wallowing in the fact that we still had no answers, when there was a knock at the door. Nobody knocks on the door when you are camping. Usually people keep to themselves. The campground was empty, except the manager and a few people scattered throughout looking to get away from the hustle and bustle of daily life. Outside the door was an older gentleman, maybe in his late seventies, who told us he heard we were a pastor's family and he came to hear our story. We were out the door in seconds, sipping on ice tea with our new visitor as he unraveled the most amazing story of who he was. He was the former president of The National Association of Evangelicals and prayer counsel to one of the president's wives, while they were in office. He said he had been in and out of the White House hundreds of times.

Now, Troy's passions are his faith, his family, and politics, so why on earth did God bring this man, who embodied all of his passions, to our door? What are the chances of us being here at the same time and why was he even here to begin with? Chance or divine appointment? It didn't matter. He was here and we were so encouraged by his visit, his wisdom, and his journey. God had sent someone to our door to encourage us and raise our arms when we were too tired to lift them. Next, we unraveled our story before him. He placed his shaky hands in ours, and with tears in his eyes, began to pray. There was such a spirit of unity and connection. We all felt it. After he prayed, he simply smiled, bid us goodbye, and shuffled off slowly up the hill. Then he turned around and declared so casually, but so matter-of-factly, "Oh, and by the way, you are on the right path." With that, our batteries were instantly recharged. It was as if God Himself was encouraging us to keep going. It's a good thing too, because Troy was getting ready to apply at Wal-Mart, because he thought he had heard God wrong and missed the boat. After that divine encounter, we had renewed strength to keep going…walking with just one foot in front of the other.

"Oh, and by the way, you are on the right path."

A God-Sized Vision

Leaving Oregon, we journeyed back to New Jersey on the northern route, thinking we were now going to somehow step into this vision God gave us while we were there. The vision involved land, soil regeneration, finances and investments, a healing center, immersions, and the nations. It was big and overwhelming. Previously, we had settled into the idea of a comfortable life of pastoring a church of a few hundred, so this new vision felt too big for us. That is exactly what it is supposed to be. If we could do it on our own, then it is not a God-sized vision. This would require faith, more character, confronting our pasts, the shedding of a lens of poverty and religious mindsets, identifying many limiting beliefs, and conquering those giants of fear and unbelief. No wonder he called us out on a journey. We had a lot of work ahead of us. We thought we were ready at the time, but realized our shoulders were not big enough to carry what He wanted to give us. **He knew the weight of the vision would crush us if we didn't have the mind of Christ to walk it out.**

After New Jersey, we stayed in South Carolina with Troy's brother, Todd. Months later we were back up to New Jersey parked in our friends Lee and Kelli's driveway for a few months, along with a mini meltdown, and then to Texas because God thought that would be a good idea. From Texas we went back to South Carolina for four years, and then "officially" back to New Jersey. There are a thousand and one stories along the way, and I will get to many of them, but what I want to stress before I get into the obstacles, is the process. You have to love the process because the process is where the magic happens. It's in the middle of the mess that you discover what you are made of. We live in a society that wants to take a pill at the first sign of a headache or wants an instant dropdown menu with a plethora of choices. We have grown accustomed to getting exactly what we want, from anywhere in the world, all within a matter of days or even overnight. To live in the magic, we can't just turn off, not answer, or ignore process.

> *"You have to love the process because the process is where the magic happens. It's in the middle of the mess that you discover what you are made of."*

Toast and Grape Jelly

Recently at church, I had started something new and was feeling insecure about it. Process can be uncomfortable because we don't always know what the outcome will be. Most things in the kitchen or home I am pretty confident in, but branching out into a new area where I may flounder for a bit, is uncomfortable. My friend George approached me with a strange prophetic word. He said, "I have four words for you that make no sense to me, but will hopefully mean something to you." He continued, "toast and grape jelly." Well, it didn't make sense in the moment, but during worship, I had a vision of a tiny white table and chairs, the kind little girls have in their bedrooms for tea. It was laid out with miniature china pieces. God was sitting at the tiny table, scrunched up on the little white chair like a daddy having a cup of tea with his daughter. I was seated at the table, as a little girl, serving him toast with grape jelly. He smiled and took such delight in His treat. Then He began to tell me that I can cook fabulous meals with the best of them, but I got my start with toast and grape jelly and He was just as pleased then as He is now. We all have to start somewhere. He is in the process and takes delight in every step. We move from victory, not for it.

Love Your Leah

Process has become as dirty a word as submission. But in the wise words of Pastor Paul Martini, Associate Pastor at Life Center in Harrisburg, PA; "You have to love your Leah. As long as Leah (the process) remains unloved, Rachel (the destination) will be barren." In the book of Genesis chapters 29-30, Rachel was the love and desired end of Jacob's life. She was the promise and Jacob's destination. He was promised Rachel, but was deceived by the uncle he worked for into marrying Leah, the unlovely sister. In her rejection, God looked down and opened her womb and she produced many children, but Rachel was barren until all the fruit had been produced through Leah. It was only then that Rachel conceived and gave birth.

In the waiting time, when you have promises from God's Word and prophetic words from His people, the enemy wants to come and sow his own seeds: seeds of doubt, fear, and unbelief. When we think we have missed the opportunity or that God has skipped over us, then we begin to settle for stones instead of bread. We become tempted to jump back in the boat or worse yet, step out of grace and start striving and performing, thinking we can get God's attention through our works. There is no way around the process, but you can become more informed, know your enemy, and most importantly know your God and His promises. Then you use those to step into the destiny He prepared for you to walk in. The process doesn't have to take as long either, if you know what to expect and how to navigate the waters.

Godly Counselors

It is important, even invaluable, to have godly counselors. But...never settle for counsel from anyone you wouldn't trade places with. Now, I am not saying you can't learn from anyone, but many people living life from inside the boat will counsel and advise you, having never stepped foot on the water themselves. They don't know where you are going because they have never been there themselves. The Holy Spirit will guide you. He is the best Counselor. You need to have someone in your court praying with you and helping you hear and discern God's voice. You will need help in how to receive a vision and interpret it. Our hope is that through our story we can help you identify and break down each obstacle, give you strategies to overcome, and tools to equip you for the journey, should you be bold enough to step out.

Once you step out of the boat, you will realize you are not alone. Jesus is right there, ready to walk this journey with you and He has placed others in your path to keep you full of faith, hope, wisdom, and encouragement. As you grow in your process, there will always be temptations, but the rebound will be quicker as you become aware of the enemy's schemes. You will know the God in front of you, enabling you to live and move from rest and belief. You will no longer battle with fear, doubt and unbelief, your past, religious mindsets, or even an immature character. Is the camper still on the road? You will wonder at times too. Obviously, the camper never fell off the road, dragging the van, and our family with it, to our death. We made it down the mountain in one piece, but it was a moment and experience we will never forget. When you submit to the process, grip the wheel, and keep your eyes focused on Jesus, even the cliffs display a beauty that you wouldn't have seen had you been blinded by fear and unbelief.

Secret #4

Don't go this journey alone. But don't take counsel from someone you wouldn't trade places with either.

Secret #5

Love the Process

CHAPTER FOUR

It was Only a Stone that Took Down a Giant: Exposing the Obstacle of Fear

One decision made from the place of doubt
or fear can easily snowball into a life half-lived.

~ Jaime Cross, CEO & Founder of MIG & the Her Effect ®

The sun had finally made its spring entrance and the gloom of overcast days were a forgotten memory. Months of pent-up energy had to find its way into a two-hour window of time in the garden. It was just one of those days when the sounds became clear and the sensations on the skin became more noticeable. Even the spring odors seemed more fragrant. I hadn't smelled Spring before with such emphasis. Fall, yes, it has its distinct aromas, but maybe I have always been too busy for Spring. Has it always been so fresh and new? Honeysuckle, wisteria, and fresh cut grass wafted on the breeze. Spring is sweet and alive.

I could feel my sun-warmed skin beginning to tighten and sting. The kids had all wandered inside and Troy and I were alone cleaning up the tools and straightening the yard. The pool called to me. I answered. I scooped a handful of water and poured it over my feet to rinse off. We had just filled the little 8ft x3ft kiddie pool, and that sparkling blue water looked so refreshing. The water was cold and had a happy, bitter bite. I love cold water. I have never understood people who wanted to heat their pools to bathwater temp to swim. When I am hot, I want to be refreshed and cooled down. This water was Lake Tahoe cold. The blue dancing waters seemed to speak memories to my mind calling out the once playful child who didn't think so much.

"I guess I could just stand in the pool," I thought. I hiked up my gardening shorts and stood in the water. The bottom cushioned my toes. I stood there thinking how wonderful it was to have a pool in my side yard for the kids to play in all summer long. But quickly another thought bullied its way to the surface.

"Just fall in."

Immediately, my adult, mom brain began to correct that wandering child's voice who needed to learn to keep her wayward feet on the ground. "You are in your work clothes. The water is cold. You have a million things to do. You need to wear a swimsuit."

"But that takes too long," the lazy child argued, "and the moment will be gone. Fall in. It is what you really want to do. So, do it. Excuses are just lies you tell yourself that keep you from what you really want. Do what you really want. Let me out. It's me, the girl who always took the dare. The girl who embraced the challenge. The one who thought, 'You say I can't? Well, watch me.' Where is she? Where is the girl who bathed in the ice melt stream on camping trips with a bar of soap and nothing but her wits? Remember the water is fine once your body is numb. And what about the girl who tackled the moguls and ran into trees skiing? The one who accidentally found herself on the black diamond side of the mountain, but oh well, knew there was only one way to get down…and that was down. Where is the girl who drove through the drive-thru backwards just because it would make a memory, not just for her, but for Anna? It would be one of those formative memories that bond two cousins together, forever. Not to mention, it would be a good laugh. Consequences, what are those? That's where that girl went. She was captured by the "enlightened consequences fairy". You know, the one who knows the possibilities of all that could happen? Is that some kind of badge you get as a mom, like a merit you earn in Royal Rangers? Why are moms' experts at what could happen? No wonder you lost yourself. You stopped taking the adventures and chancing the outcomes to delight."

With that, I fell forward and just let the freezing water envelop me as I let out a happy shrill from the cold. "It's freezing!" I yelled, at the top of my lungs. But I laid there in the water, completely aware of myself and the girl that had now emerged.

"Here I am," the girl announced. "Smell the sunscreen and chlorine. Doesn't it take you back to hot summer days by Mema and Papa's pool; sliding down the slide, swimming under water with opened eyes and only the muffled sounds of happy voices from above? You felt alive under the water. Remember how you just wanted to strip off all your clothes and swim uninhibited without boarders like a mermaid? You were a mermaid, so wild and free with your long curls dancing under the water. Then you would lay out on a towel on the hot concrete and the warm California sun would cover you like a blanket. All you thought about was swimming and lunch and that happy smile that just stuck to your face because you just loved life. Remember her? Look at the trees and how they sway back and forth in the wind with their gentle rising and falling whispers. What are they saying? Everything speaks around you. Tune in and hear the voice of life. It's all worship. The birds, the sun, the trees, and your cold scream. He loves to see you fully alive. That is when the glory descends. There's that smile on your face. That grateful to be alive smile that shines from deep inside. I have been locked inside waiting to be set free. Free to dream. Free to take risks and join life's advancing adventure call. I don't want to be stuck behind a sink of dirty dishes or piles of laundry all of the time. I want my voice to be heard. I want to have a voice again. I want to sing and laugh and scream with delight. I want to lead you into who you really are, the one you have buried under all those suppose-tos. I have been suffocating. Thank you for letting me out. Now, I can speak and feel and listen and tell you what I see and feel and hear. I want to show you what others refuse to see because their voices are also buried. Excuses are lies that bury people under mediocre, half-baked lives. Learn to listen and respond and know that the excuses you hear are only keeping you from bliss. The enemy is a thief and a liar. You would have cooled your feet, but you would have missed the release, the wonder, the smile, the 'I just did this.' You would have missed you."

"You would have missed you."

Who Told You That?

The journey stripped us of everything. I had started down that path toward mediocrity, settling for what I thought was next in life. Life doesn't have to be about the next thing. I am not talking about dreaming of the future, but rather the rut we buy into when we just surrender to what our future brings, instead of making it happen. We think college comes after high school; a 9-5 job follows after college; retirement begins at 65. Who told you that? I had lost my spark for a while, because I didn't know how to stretch the imagination and dream bigger. I was comfortable with "middle of the rock" except for that inner voice that kept calling me up; calling me up to live beyond myself. Children have a natural ability to dream and enjoy life without all the weight of responsibility. We lose that free-spirited zest for life if we are not careful. I had surrendered to age as if my prime was over, but truthfully, what I had really surrendered to was fear. I knew I had dreams buried, but for one reason or another, I pushed down the possibilities with my excuses. To be fully alive also meant to be fully surrendered and vulnerable; fully exposed and risking disappointment.

Partnering with Fear

There are five obstacles I want to present to you that we will all face as we step out of the boat. The first is fear. Fear is the number one issue we deal with in our prayer ministry and the number one cause of mediocrity. Fear partners with the flesh and whispers his lies and excuses, disguised as protection and comfort. Fear robs us of those moments of pure bliss. Although fear is the issue that brings most people to us, the root is always a distorted view of God and His love, and a distorted view of ourselves. Most everything comes down to belief, but because fear is what we feel, I want to address it separately. Fear starts as a feeling, which then triggers doubt and unbelief. It is actually a spirit that tries to get us to partner with the emotion so he can wreak havoc in our souls. When we partner with fear, our anxiety and worry are his worship. Through our worship, he gains the power to cripple and distract, to weaken and destroy, and cause us to shrink and to hide, but only *if* we allow him that power. Fear has been defined as: False Evidence Appearing Real - F.E.A.R. I love this definition because it unmasks the demon and lays his identity bare before us. He is an illusion.

"False Evidence Appearing Real - F.E.A.R."

On our journey, fear was the most crippling emotion we encountered. Fear manifests in many forms. Sometimes we felt afraid for our lives. Other times we were afraid because we felt inadequate. Fear is all about self-preservation by projecting negative scenarios that, in my opinion, 99% of the time never happen. Fear was often followed by guilt and doubt. Guilt for feeling fear when we should be having faith, and doubt because the pictures he paints can have some truth to them, but it gets twisted. This is why it is important to declare truth over your life, not facts. The most important weapon for fighting fear is Love. The Bible says in 1 John 4:18, *"There is no fear in love; but perfect love casts out fear, because fear involves torment. But he who fears has not been made perfect in love."* This verse is not talking about being loving, it's about knowing Love intimately. God is love. When we live loved and know our God, there is nothing that can touch us. We become like Whom we behold. The more time we spend with God, through His Word and in His presence through worship, or stepping out in faith and trust, the more we become like Him. The opposite is true too. When we spend time meditating on fearful images, saturated by fearful music and movies, or entertain fearful thoughts that the enemy places in our mind, we become fearful. If there were two dogs on your shoulder, one fear and one love, and they were battling for the throne of your heart, who would win? The answer is the one fed the most.

The 23rd Psalm

God leads us to love through His Word and His Spirit. Jesus lived loved and that is reflected in His life. He walked in absolute peace with no fear. I love Psalm 23 in the Passion Translation, which says;

> The Lord is my best friend and my shepherd. I always have more than enough. He offers a resting place for me in His luxurious love. His tracks take me to an oasis of peace, the quiet brook of bliss. That's where He restores and revives my life. He opens before me pathways to God's pleasure and leads me along in His footsteps of righteousness so that I can bring honor to His name. Lord, even when your path takes me through the valley of deepest darkness, fear will never conquer me, for you already have! You remain close to me and lead me through it all the way. Your authority is my strength and my peace. The comfort of your love takes away my fear. I'll never be lonely, for you are near. You become my delicious feast even when my enemies dare to fight. You anoint me with the fragrance of your Holy Spirit; you give me all I can drink of you until my heart overflows. So why would I fear the future? For your goodness and love pursue me all the days of my life. Then afterward, when my life is through, I'll return to your glorious presence to be forever with you!

I love The Passion Translation because it expounds on the text through the lens of the Father's love. You can hear His heart, passion, and emotion in the text. Different translations help bring more depth and perspective to the voice of His Word. I recommend reading from several translations, in large portions, to frame your context and gather a big picture. For example, in other translations it refers to His rod and staff bringing comfort or His Word and Spirit bringing comfort. By combining several translations, the image broadens. Now I have a picture of the rod and authority being His Word and sometimes bringing needed correction. The staff and His love being the Spirit, bringing comfort. The authority of the Word of God becomes my protection and His Spirit of love leads me like a staff on the path. What an amazing picture.

Hidden Treasures

My family, including my parents and siblings and their families, journeyed to the beautiful Oregon coast for a camping trip to celebrate Abby's first birthday when we were living in Oregon. While combing the rocks on the coastline, my brother made a discovery. He found rounded glass stones up on a rock. It was an odd thing to find at the beach, although Oregon is known for their beach glass. This wasn't beach glass though; it was those little glass pieces you find in the bottom of flower vases. In colors of blue, green and white, we discovered them in such odd places, like tucked away on the tops of massive boulders out in the ocean. These boulders were usually surrounded by water, except at low tide. We all started scavenging for them. We found nine in total, and then no more. It was a finding frenzy at first and then nothing. It was almost as if God wanted us to find nine and that was it. They were treasures from heaven and had some prophetic meaning, I was sure.

I am always looking because she who has eyes to see, sees. In California, my son Caleb found a white one buried in my mom's garden. My mom doesn't use things like that, so I thought it was strange. He found the eleventh on a piece of property we had fallen in love with, perfect for the vision, in Virginia, in the closet of an empty house. The twelfth, was a pink one in Georgia, on a nightstand of a friend's house. He found it and asked if he could have it. My friend said she had never seen it before and wondered where it came from. This was Caleb's and my game of hide-and-seek. He loved searching for the hidden treasures.

The thirteenth stone was miraculous. I believed they all were, but this one in particular gave me no doubt. My daughter and I had felt led to clean out the nursery of the church we attended while living in Fort Mill, SC. All Nations Church, led by Pastors Mahesh and Bonnie Chavda, was a church walking in Kingdom revival, but we had noticed the nursery was no place for the next generation to play. The atmosphere was not congruent with the message spoken from the pulpit. It was more of a storage closet of people's old hand-me-downs that they couldn't part with at the Goodwill, so they donated them to the church nursery. It was disorganized and the atmosphere felt oppressive. I felt a poverty spirit and wanted to cleanse the place by removing all the old and worthless items. It was also a prophetic act of what we were doing in our own lives, cleansing our beliefs of a poverty mindset. We wanted to rid ourselves of anything not useful for the road ahead. We gutted, cleaned, organized, stocked and prayed over the building the children would be in. I could feel the poverty spirit had gone. It was now a welcoming place with a pleasant atmosphere. Ashley finished vacuuming and I prayed over both rooms when all of a sudden, we looked down on the carpet she had just vacuumed, and found the thirteenth stone. This one had what looked like a dove or angel inside. We had just vacuumed and this was not something usually found in a nursery. It was a choking hazard. No, this one was placed there strategically by an angel. God was pleased with the cleansing and the removing of the poverty spirit.

The fourteenth stone I found just before we left South Carolina on our way back to New Jersey. This stone had a flame in the center. We knew that our time at All Nations Church had equipped us with many tools. We received impartations from many great and anointed prophets, pastors, healing evangelists, teachers, and apostles as they laid hands on, prayed, and prophesied over us. Pastors Mahesh and Bonnie had become spiritual parents to us and we knew that by partnering with them, we entered into their anointing as their spiritual children. They had covered us in prayer and prophesied into our lives for over four years. We were leaving with fire and this fire stone was a testament to that truth.

The last stone we found in New Jersey. There are fifteen in total. We started finding them in Oregon with all nine at once, ending in New Jersey with fifteen. We started this journey in 2009 and arrived in New Jersey for the last leg of the preparation in 2015. It is no coincidence. It was like He was leaving love notes all over for us to find. The message was that we were not alone on this journey. We knew we had angels watching over us and leading us to things Papa would put together in the end. There was no need to fear.

"He was leaving love notes all over for us to find."

The Incredible Journey

What child gets to celebrate their first birthday in the Seattle Space Needle eating a Royal Orbitor (hot fudge sundae) served on a bed of dry ice? Hot fudge sundaes are my favorite dessert and to be served one completely engulfed in an icy fog was out of this world. What a journey we were on, getting the chance to see the country together as a family. It was a homeschool dream. I remember feeling guilty that my children didn't have a normal life with piano lessons and baseball games, until I realized that not many children get to study Laura Ingles Wilder books, and then not only visit the prairie where the Little House books took place, but have the whole homestead to themselves for an entire day and night. We had enjoyed a show at Sight and Sound Theatre in Lancaster, Pennsylvania, almost drowned at the Titanic Museum in Branson, Missouri, delighted in the spirit of excellence at the Creation Museum in Kentucky, and went back in time at Lincoln's New Salem, and the Presidential Museum in Springfield, Illinois. We witnessed grizzly bears and buffalo up close in Yellowstone, basked in the falls in Yosemite, panned for gold and had our stagecoach robbed by masked bandits in Columbia, California, conversed with a real mountain man in the Smokey Mountains, watched the sun set on Mount Rushmore, played the washboard at a cowboy dinner show, and so many more memories that fill our Shutterfly albums. The children are always pouring through the albums and reminiscing together. It was an incredible journey.

The Fear of the Lord and an Open Heaven

One such encounter happened on a morning in Yellowstone; a day I would gain a proper understanding of the fear of the Lord versus the obstacle of fear. We had been in Yellowstone for three days and today was the day we were going to see the Sulphur pits, specifically the Grand Prismatic Spring. It is so large and colorful it can be seen from space. We awoke to rain, which meant the pits would not be as visible or their colors at their peak. I was disappointed at first until I realized this was what I was looking forward to and the enemy was not going to steal it from me. In my Spirit I felt like God whispered that I was to take authority over the weather. He gives us the desires of our heart, doesn't He? I declared and released an open heaven over the geyser area. Hey, He said in Genesis we were to take dominion. I think He likes His children to take Him at His word. I wasn't ordering God around; I was only speaking out loud what His Word already declared. I was speaking what I heard Him say, just like Jesus did. I had never done this myself, but had heard stories.

In the Bible, Jesus calmed the storms and the waves. He said we would do even greater things…so why not? Driving through the rain to the geyser area, we arrived at our destination, only to find an oval of blue sky, a literal open heaven where once the area was engulfed in rain. I snapped a picture to document my miracle. An open heaven… God is so amazing! We walked along the boardwalk in such delight and witnessed the beautiful colors. These pits were enormous. Troy took the children on ahead, while I lingered at the Grand Prismatic Spring. It was so enormous that it literally made me afraid. All my insides felt like Jell-O. Kind of like that feeling you get while standing on the edge of a cliff and you get this strange urge to jump. Is that just me? I felt in awe of its great size and power. It was like looking into the eye of God. I couldn't see all of it because of the fog, which added to its mystery, but knowing what was out there, gripped me with such reverential fear I can only explain it as a fraction of what it must feel like to encounter God face to face.

I felt like I was looking at His face and part of me felt I would disintegrate in His presence. Then all of a sudden, I was engulfed in the fog and I could feel the breath of God all around me whispering my name on each cheek, above me and behind me. Although it was not the name Rebecca, it was a name that I somehow knew was mine, a name I must be called in heaven. My knees were weak and I started to cry. I was being engulfed in His presence. Fear of God is the only fear that is permissible. The Bible tells us in Proverbs 9:10 that *"the fear of the Lord is the beginning of wisdom, and the knowledge of the Holy One is understanding."* I can tell you that in that moment I felt fear, but not the kind of runaway fear that puts distance between you and God, but rather the kind of fear that makes you feel so small and yet engulfed in such big hands. The fear of the Lord is about having the right perspective of who you are compared to Who He is.

"The fear of the Lord is about having the right perspective of who you are compared to Who He is."

Joseph and the Fear of Inadequacy

It was the most amazing experience to camp across the country and move our house on wheels wherever we felt led. One particular week we pulled into Redding, California to visit Bethel Church and attend their Supernatural School of Worship for children. I stayed with our three-year-old Shanna in her class. This one afternoon, one of the youth leaders performed a dance with swords. He was a strong and muscular young man, so full of innocence. He stood there with the lights dimmed and two swords, one in each hand. Before he began, he blessed us to see what God wanted us to see. I was so new to the prophetic world. I felt as if I was amongst giants at Bethel; I was there to learn and observe. The music began. He picked a song titled "Holy," by Matt Gilman. He stood poised with the swords folded across his chest when the music began.

Immediately I was taken to a different place. I was having an open vision. The young man, whose name is Joseph, immediately grew giant-sized and he rose above the earth until it was a small speck below him. His entire performance took place in the heavens, as he warred and wielded his swords. I saw a Scripture passage run through my mind: Daniel 10, describing the heavenly battle between Michael the archangel of heaven and the principality over Persia. Daniel had been interceding, but his answer was delayed twenty-one days due to the battle in the heavenlies. As I watched Joseph swing his swords in this choreographed dance, I somehow knew that when he danced, he was interceding in the heavenlies.

God was giving me His perspective of our worship. When we prayed, danced, or worshipped it wasn't just bouncing off the ceiling. Our worship is powerful. We are more spirit than flesh and the spirit realm is real. This vision blew my religious background right out of the water. I had no idea what was going on when I worshipped or prayed. Now, I don't wield a physical sword in a dance, but my declarations and worship shifts atmospheres, releases angels, and moves the heart of God. Truthfully, we carry the Holy Spirit, so we can't help but shift atmospheres wherever we tread. When the song ended, I sat there stunned thinking everyone must have observed the same open vision. The lights came on and people clapped and continued on to the next activity planned. I couldn't move. I stared at Joseph wondering if he knew what had just happened. Immediately God spoke to me and told me to tell him. I argued that this was Bethel, so of course he knew. He wasn't going to hear it from me; a housewife from New Jersey. This was nothing more than the fear of man. Fear of man robs you of encounters with God and robs others of the answers to their prayers. I had decided I would let someone more "spiritual" tell him. This argument went on for 3 days. I felt so inexperienced and inadequate, that I must have made it up. He would probably look at me and say, "Thanks lady. Have a nice day. You have quite an imagination."

Finally, I couldn't take it anymore and I timidly approached this well-seasoned spiritual warrior and said, "Excuse me. I have been in an argument with God the past three days and I just need to settle this so I can sleep." I began to relay the vision I had before him. His body resonated with the words I was speaking. He teared up and couldn't believe what I was saying. Excited, he exclaimed, "I have been asking God for months to please tell me what happens when I dance. My middle name is Daniel so your Scripture resonates with me. I feel so compelled to dance, but never knew why or what was going on. Now I do. Thank you." The interchange between us was so powerful. I felt the presence of God and was so amazed that He had used this housewife from New Jersey to answer this young man's prayer. My eyes had been opened to the spiritual realities of warfare and I had stepped out of the boat and took a risk to speak a vision over a stranger and it changed both our lives. We don't always get it right, but there is no greater feeling when we do and we touch a life. It takes practice. Your gift makes room for you. All those "practice" times, when we may be off in our prophetic words, we get to touch God. He loves to see His children take risks, step out in faith, and live life from His vantage point.

"Your gift makes room for you."

Captain of Angel Armies

The best way to battle fear is to get God's perspective on things. In the account of 2 Kings 6, Elisha prayed that his servant's eyes would be opened to see that greater was the invisible angelic army of horses and chariots of fire surrounding them, than the enemy he witnessed with his own physical eyes. I, too, have asked Him to reveal Himself to me in specific ways. For instance, I read that Jesus is the Captain of Angel Armies. What does that look like? I asked Him to use my imagination, which He gave me, to paint a picture of what that looked like. He immediately opened up a vision of Him on a throne with thousands of angels with bright and heavy swords in their hands. There were angels as far as the eye could see. They were stomping their feet on the ground ready for battle, and the sound thundered and echoed through the great throne room. He was brilliant light and so enormous and terrifying. Yet, I felt His strength and power, knowing if He was on my side, what chance did the enemy have? The vision so overwhelmed me and gave me such confidence. It put in perspective my place of authority and Who has my back. These heavenly hosts are ministering spirits drawn to truth and the power of His words released from our mouths. They work in alignment with God's truth…not our facts. I asked for a vision who He was as the Captain of Angel Armies and this perspective changed my life. Fear lost a huge grip with that image. Now, I remind myself and my children who the Captain of Angel Armies is and that He is here for us.

Know Truth, Know Your Normal, and Speak Right Words

Fearful spirits exude fear. They are afraid. 1 Peter 5:8 warns; "*Be sober, be vigilant; because your adversary the devil walks about like a roaring lion, seeking whom he may devour.*" This is not a Scripture given to produce fear because 2 Timothy 1:7 declares, "*For God has not given us a spirit of fear, but of power, and of love and of a sound mind.*" We are not defensive in the Kingdom. We are offensive. Here the Word declares that we have love, power, and a sound mind as our weapons. There is an enemy who studies us looking for our weak spots, but when we walk in the truth of who we are, the enemy can't touch us. We need to watch our words, because what we speak is what we believe. We need to speak the truth. But to speak the truth, you must know the truth. Truth is a person. The more intimately you know Him and walk in unity with Him, the less of a target you are and more of a threat you become. In truth, **the enemy trembles in the presence of a believer who knows who they are in Christ**. When a believer embraces their true identity, then the enemy's identity is revealed, devastating all his plans. I would rather be a threat than a target. How about you?

I am learning to walk in truth by declaring the truth out loud so my mind hears it. I love how Romans 10:17 encourages us, *"Faith comes by hearing, and hearing by the Word of God."* Not only can we find encouragement from the written, "logos" Word of God, but in this verse, the word "Word" in the Greek is "rhema". A rhema is when the Lord speaks His own word a second time. It is a living word, a "now" word, because He is alive. It is a word from His Word for you specifically. When we speak His written Word as well as His rhema's, we are actually releasing His will and His breath on this earth. The more we speak the truth and release His breath, the more faith we will walk in. This is warfare and the Word of God is your sword. Sharpen it and know how to wield it.

Become aware of your "normal" so that you can learn to govern your atmosphere. I am usually excessively positive and joyful, so taking offense is not normal. If we don't govern our atmosphere, we can assume an emotion is ours instead of recognizing it as the enemy's. For example, fear is an unpleasant spirit masquerading as an emotion brought on by a belief that someone or something is dangerous, will cause pain, or is a threat to us. I have encountered fear and have allowed him to mentor me on more than one occasion, until I realized I was just opening my mind to dreaming with the devil. When the enemy can get us to come into agreement with his lies and speak them out, he has gained ground in our lives and can start building his fortress.

Fear, or any spirit for that matter, only has the power we give it through our words and beliefs. Fear wants to distract you from knowing your identity and from hearing the truth. It does this by painting fearful scenarios of the unknown, bringing up past failures, projecting a dark future, threatening rejection, disappointment, pain, poverty, loss of control, as well as false images of the true character of God. He will stop at nothing to project any scenario that will derail you and get you to step off the path God has for you. He will lie to you and twist the truth. He will project a Goliath in front of you and remind you that you have nothing but stones to throw. What he doesn't want you to believe is that those stones, when breathed on by God, are the exact weapons that can bring down our enemies. I love what James Goll says, "If God allows a Goliath in front of you, then He knows there is a David inside of you." Do you see how important belief and identity are in slaying our enemies?

> ## "If God allows a Goliath in front of you, then He knows there is a David inside of you."

Handcuffed by a Vow

My biggest fear growing up was ending up poor, in a cardboard box of a house, out in the middle of nowhere. My fear of the future left me wide open to vows I would make apart from God. This is simply idolatry, self-preservation, and thinking I knew better than God what was good for my own life. When I was younger, I vowed I would never be poor. My life was motivated by my fear of poverty. I grew up a latch key kid and was old enough to watch the very real struggles of a single mother. Not only did I subconsciously learn the message that a woman was dependent on a man if she was to find happiness, security, and yes, even money, but I believed the lie that God was not out for my success or happiness, He just wanted my holiness. When we make confessions with our mouths or vows apart from God, we cuff His hands and end up sowing into our futures the exact opposite of what we hope for. Our words of fear, judgement, pride, and self-protection are seeds we sow into the spiritual realm that end up bearing the wrong fruit. We may end up getting exactly what we hoped for, only it comes with the cost of our freedom. I didn't know I could give my fears to God, remove the cuffs I had placed on Him, and allow Him to lead me to a life of pursuing the dreams He placed in my heart in the first place.

Instead of opening my heart to the One who could comfort and supply, I pushed Him away and vowed to go at life on my own terms. I still believed in Him and wanted to please Him, but this area I locked away and kept Him at a distance. Fear painted a picture of my future that kept me on the wrong side of the tracks as a helpless victim. The only way out, according to my very limited understanding, was to marry a wealthy man to ensure my security, or at the very least, one who had ambitions of wealth. Now, I didn't think this consciously, but that image locked me into a path I would pursue at any cost. Don't ask me why I never thought I could become wealthy on my own. I wanted to be a wife and a mother, so to me, there was no way of making my own money. It was just not something that was modeled for me or even a concept in my limited thinking. Fear was quick to present himself as my protector and provider and he gave me an identity to strive after so I wouldn't end up poor. **I was a prisoner to my dream rather than a participant in my own life.** This vow severely limited God in how He wanted to place good things into my life to *"prosper me and not to harm me"* (see Jeremiah 29:11). Marrying a pastor wasn't part of my plans, because in my experience, pastors were poor and dependent —everything I didn't want to be. Gotta love those limiting beliefs.

It should be no surprise that when we arrived in Texas, halfway through our journey, still living in a camper, my husband making peanuts for a salary, and me now pregnant with number five, I realized I had reached the vortex of my greatest fear. I had ended up in a glorified cardboard box, and to boot, out in the middle of nowhere, far away from everything. I stared at our camper realizing the power of my words and beliefs and yet His grace whispered over me in that moment that my situation was not who I am. My experience was not my identity. I was the same person whether I lived in a castle or a cardboard box. I was loved and His treasure, and what fear had projected was only half the truth. I was surrounded by the people I loved the most, and although I didn't want to remain in this situation, I was okay. I repented of the vow I had made and gave my financial future to God. I knew He was good and I knew He had amazing dreams for me to pursue. Those dreams would cost money so I also had to reconcile a few beliefs I had about God and money, and **lay aside what I had been taught for what the Bible really says.** Fear is a liar and he twists the truth. Know the Word of God, for it is our sword and faith is our shield.

Facts vs. Truth

Fear not only had his talons in me, but he was doing his work in my children as well. My daughter Ashley missed the life we had back in New Jersey. She missed her climbing trees, her friends, and the security a home brings to a little one. While living in our camper in our friend's driveway for a few weeks, she was really struggling with lies. She relayed to us that one afternoon, while taking a walk, she had felt claws gripping her shoulders. She heard voices telling her that she was going to be homeless, and this vision that God gave us was a joke and was never going to happen. She spoke out loud, "In Jesus's name, go away." It left, but not without first planting a seed of doubt in her mind. After all, the facts were that we were wandering around in a camper. The facts were that we were running out of money and still had not known how to step into the vision God had given us. The truth is, facts are our reality, but they are not always truth. Charles Capps put it powerfully in his tiny book, *God's Creative Power* (pp7-9):

> *My people are void of speech. They hear the world and speak as the world speaks. By observing circumstances, they have lost sight of my word. They even speak that which the enemy says, and they destroy their own inheritance by corrupt communication of fear and unbelief. No word of mine is void of power, only powerless when unspoken.*

He goes on to say, "Confess victory in the face of apparent defeat. Confess abundance in the face of apparent lack." It is not denying what is in front of us; it is *"giving life to the dead and calling those things which do not exist as though they did"* (Romans 4:17). It is learning to declare God's truth and speak into existence what He says in exchange for the present reality. When we pray the Lord's Prayer found in Matthew Chapter 6, we confess, *"Your Kingdom come. Your will be done on earth as it is in heaven."* As believers, do we really believe what we are declaring or are we just making a mental agreement and speaking empty words into the cosmos?

Listen to the songs you sing. Don't sing them if you don't believe them and if you don't believe them ask why.

"...facts are our reality, but they are not always truth."

A Sixty Second Thought Inventory

Get in touch with the thoughts that roam around in your head and discern who is speaking. Write it down if you must. Take 60 seconds and record every thought that runs through your head and then analyze how much time you devote to the voice of God versus the voice of the enemy or the flesh. We may think we are thinking godly thoughts most of the time, but have you ever truly tested it? Which voice is louder? Is it the flesh? The enemy? Holy Spirit? Your perfect spirit-man? Get curious with what really goes on in your head instead of allowing it to be a place where the enemy runs wild without you even being aware. How do you know whose voice is whose? Holy Spirit draws, comforts, teaches and encourages. He is patient and will always sound like He is described in Scripture through the person of Jesus. If you can't hear Jesus saying it, then it probably isn't God. Your perfect Spirit-man will confirm what the Holy Spirit believes. The flesh is constantly focused on the self and wants to protect itself, usually by resorting to comfort and safety. The enemy drives and points fingers. He accuses, puts you down, is judgmental, and leaves you feeling discouraged, hopeless, fearful, and condemned. Who are you listening to? Remember, you are powerful. If you are born again, you are a new creation in Christ and you do hear God speak.

Don't let the enemy tell you differently. Remind the flesh that he is a dead man on a victorious cross and remind the enemy that he is a defeated foe.

Capps urges us to speak and declare out loud God's truth so that we hear what we are saying. Speak it until you believe it. God told Capps, "I have told my people they can have what they say, but they are saying what they have." When Ashley encountered that lying spirit, we responded with the truth from God's Word and declared the opposite of what the enemy had tried to plant in her heart. We read His promises. We spoke His truth. We also declared the specific words spoken over Ashley's life that speak of her destiny and calling. This practice became key in dealing with the enemy's lies. The weapons that we use are not the weapons of this world, but of the Kingdom. We use His Word like a sword, entering into rest, believing that what He says He will do, because He is faithful and does not lie.

"I have told my people they can have what they say, but they are saying what they have."

Fear of Lack and the Tyranny of Performance

During our time in South Carolina, we incurred a great debt in order to keep food on the table. I am not talking about frivolous spending. We used our credit cards for needs and occasionally our wants. Troy's job, although it helped, was not enough to sustain a family of eight. We were still learning how to walk in breakthrough. We didn't understand the debt. Truthfully, we didn't understand money or God's perspective on wealth and prosperity. We didn't know God as our Provider. Our financial situation seemed a contradiction to His Word and His promises. We knew the issue was not with Him, but in our beliefs. When it came to money, we still lived as orphans with a lens of poverty. I believed it was up to us and no matter what hoops we jumped through, albeit self-imposed, we couldn't find the way out of debt, which left us disillusioned. Our theology was formed out of our disappointments and experiences, rather than knowing how to steward truth in the midst of our circumstances. We were seeing fruitfulness in every area of our lives except financially, which meant what we believed about money was not in line with the Kingdom. Our minds needed a new belief about money because what we were doing was not working.

Fear gripped me when it came to money because I was afraid of debt. I was still afraid of being poor. God told me that it was His debt and it was paid for. But then why did we still owe it? He promised there would be provision at the end of the journey, but I felt that end was totally up to us and that we were somehow still drowning because we hadn't said the right words, fasted enough, or sown enough seeds. You name it. We did it. Remember how I told you if you don't understand grace, when things get tough, you will resort to performance, striving, and legalism? Debt was something I could not understand. If God was a good Father, why were we in debt? Well, He is a good Father and we didn't have the full picture. It is in those testing times that we discover what we really believe. He told me that if He paid it off before I was ready, then I would always be afraid of debt. We want God to deliver us from the darkness, but sometimes to do that would cripple us because we would forever be afraid of the dark. Remember my greatest fear was being poor and dependent. My security was still in money in the bank, and what I really needed to learn was that God was my unending source of provision. He is a good Father that cares for His children, but I didn't trust that. Trusting God with my finances was my locked closet. Because I had vowed to never be poor, I didn't know how to trust a Father to care for me. I had tied His hands and placed the responsibility on my own shoulders to get us out of the debt we were in. We didn't know what else to do. Thank God for credit cards and generous friends and family that were His provision for us during that interim time, as we worked out the truth of His Word.

I had believed I had somehow failed God through my performance. I recently heard a story that silenced my shame on the debt that we carried. The story referred to a man, high up in his company, that accidentally made a five-hundred-thousand-dollar mistake. In shame, he went to hand in his resignation because he knew he had cost his boss a great deal of money. The president of the company does not accept his resignation, foreseeing the mistake as simply an expensive investment in that individual. He knew the lesson had been learned. He invested in his company by investing in the young man. After all, he had billions of dollars. What was $500K to him? Pocket change. Our heavenly Father owns the cattle on a thousand hills. What was my measly little debt to him but pocket change? I had spent our journey focused on what I could not repay in my own strength, rather than focused on the God who was building His Kingdom and found me to be a worthy investment. I could no more pay our financial debt than I could pay my sin debt. It was not by anything I did, but because of everything Jesus did. God is patient, and thankfully, He is more concerned with getting to our hearts than He is about the pennies from His pocket we are spending.

"It was not by anything I did, but because of everything Jesus did."

Our Loaves and Fish

I remember praying for the money to pay off the credit card for one month. I gave the bill to God and asked Him for the money. The next night, Troy came home from church and handed me an envelope from a lady with enough money to cover the bill. She told him to tell me that I was to do with it whatever I wanted. That struck me funny that those were her exact words because as soon as he said them to me, a family came to my mind that was having difficulty putting food on the table. My heart wanted to give them the money. They needed it more than us. Led by the Spirit, Troy and I decided to do something we had never done before. Using the example in Scripture when Jesus fed the five thousand, we lifted up the check, gave thanks for provision, and decided to ask God to multiply it instead. We gave Him our loaves and fishes. We gave Him what was in our hands. We could have paid a bill and been fine for a month, but our hearts decided to give even though we were hurting financially. This doesn't make sense in the natural and I am sure many financial gurus would advise against it. We shouldn't plant our bread money or eat our seed money, unless of course, God tells you to. That is why it is so important to know His voice. The closer you become with God, the more you begin to sound alike. Your heart begins to want the same things. You will know His voice when you feel peace and move from rest. We get it wrong sometimes, but I would rather give, trusting, than withhold in fear. He can even bless our mistakes. All I know is that I really felt led to step out in faith. I wasn't trying to get my needs met by sowing a seed. He had met our need as He was doing every month and I knew He would meet this need again as well. I really believe God wanted me to know He is the source of our provision. He was providing for this bill through this woman, but I felt like He was also giving me a choice. I wanted to move by His Spirit. I was compelled by love. The next day, I delivered the money to the family. A week later, we received a check for more than ten times the amount we had sown. Heaven loves to strongly support a cheerful giver. If things become tough financially, sometimes it's just good to give to someone else. It removes the power money may have on you. Be led by His Spirit and err on the side of generosity. God does. God will give provision for the vision. Give it to Him. He takes better care of things than we ever could.

Checking Out

I love it when He gives us those little surprises that boost our faith. We need those in the wilderness times, but we are not meant to live in that struggle. The wilderness time is a school. Sometimes the lessons were hard to bear and I was so thankful for a heavenly Father I could run to Who would help me make sense of my heart and situation. I want to share an excerpt from my journal from a day I was struggling with how to see my husband and help him overcome his fear. He had been escaping through video games to a world where he could conquer and fight the battles he didn't know how to fight in real life. He was checking out. As a result, I felt rejected and abandoned. Troy had employed everything he knew to do and there was still little fruit to show for it. He was running around like an orphan trying to get our needs met. We both were. He didn't know what else to do but wait. I remember referring to this time as what it must have felt like to be in the lifeboats of the Titanic, watching the ship go down, waiting for help to arrive, that never came. When you get to the core of your beliefs, brought to the surface through trials, sometimes it can be unbearable to face. I am thankful in spite of it all, I could go to God. I always knew that His perspective was all I needed to face what was in front of me. I love talking to God because He will never play the part of the accuser. It is just not in His nature. He already sees us as perfect through Christ, but He can somehow still see us in the process as we fight *from* victory not *for* it.

"...we fight from victory not for it."

Quiet Time Reflection

Me: Papa, I am struggling with how to see Troy and I need your eyes. How do You see him?

God: I see a man who is building my foundation. He loves my law and takes delight in my statutes (rules). He is an overcomer, but does not see himself that way because you cannot see yourself clearly when you are hiding behind a wall. He will learn to come to me with His feelings. He is afraid of them. Afraid of what will come up and out and he won't be able to put the top back on. It is a terribly naked feeling and he does not yet trust Me to hold his heart. He doesn't come to Me because he believes I am not talking. But the truth is he doesn't come to Me because he has convinced himself he knows what I am going to say. He has Me all boxed up. His heart has been broken too many times with things he doesn't understand and in order to survive he has learned to think in black and white and has made no room for gray. Boxed up truths are easier to follow and don't require much risk. To risk the heart by entering into relationship costs too much and fear has been his comforter for so long. Oh, he wants to risk. He longs for the adventure. He will have it once he learns to let go. Fear is a crippling spirit. His voice is loud and arguments convincing. He coddles the flesh and deceives you into believing he will give you what you want - comfort and protection and yes, even intimacy. But in the end, he is a thief and robs you of your destiny, twists and distorts your intimacy, and blinds you to your heart's true desire. He builds the flesh and tears down the spirit. He locks you behind bars and renders you a victim to life and then blames it on Me. I have come so that he will have life and life more abundantly. Any area where there is not abundant life is locked behind a cage of lies. Fear works with blame to keep him safe and keep everyone and everything at a distance. If it is the fault of others, then there is nothing he can do and thus the cycle of fear and blame continues. Fear keeps him a victim of his circumstances. Fear has lied to him by blaming things on Me. I can't be trusted. If I can't be trusted, I can't be followed. If I can't be followed, then he needs to find his own way. So, he creates boxes and principles. It has the appearance of faith, but it is empty rules without Me. I am not saying he does not have faith or even that he is not faithful. He is faithful and he is full of faith. But he is gun-shy to test it out. He has just enough faith to get by, but the 'more' is happening all around him. I have so much more for him. He wants the more, but that takes risk and he believes he risks alone. He stands as My accuser waiting for Me to fail because the enemy has filled his head with lies. There is evidence in his hands, but he has not let Me have a turn on the stand. He knows what I am going to say because the enemy has already prepped him. So, he has his defense ready. I have been on trial ever since his dad died. Life is a trial where he must have the last word. Because that is safe and predictable. It is easier to follow. It's like discernment. As Christians you can discern something, put it into your box and respond appropriately--the way you are supposed to. The way you have been trained. The way the box says. That is religion. It is predictable, manageable and can be followed. Mankind loves to do this with my principles. But...the Kingdom walk, the walk by My spirit...this discerns and asks. The key is to ask and not assume. **Assuming is a relationship that is self-sustained**. In essence, it is a dead relationship with yourself regurgitating old conversations. Asking is inviting Me into life. Seeing what I am seeing. Saying what I am saying. The Spirit walk is a fresh walk every day. I do a new thing every time. I am not predictable, but my character never changes. How I express Myself changes. I am the same yesterday, today, and forever, but I do different things. I don't change, but in order to know My heart, he must ask. He must invite Me to be Myself. He thinks he has Me figured out and that is that I can't be figured out. That is true to a point. Every relationship in order to be alive must move and have mystery, but My heart can always be trusted because I am always out for his best. I am good. He wants to believe this, but in order to believe it he has to get rid of the accusations and the assumptions. There is no truth in them. Let Me on the stand and I will dismantle each lie one by one. But he needs to be willing to have a new paradigm. I am not who he thinks I am. I Am that I Am.

Me: What is my role?

God: Know this is not about you. He is not rejecting you. He is rejecting Me. He is rejecting those things he cannot understand or box up. Just love him through this and trust Me. He is angry because life is not fitting into its boxes anymore. He is not angry at you. His heart issues are with Me. Don't take his stuff on you. Let Me take it. You were not meant to hold it. Just hold him. Draw him out and show him your arms are safe. Allow Me to love him through you. Don't correct his thoughts or answer for him. Let him discover what he thinks and point him back to Me. Draw out his heart with questions. Not statements. Just be vulnerable and love selflessly. I am in this. I've got this. I've got him. I love you both so dearly. You will have your promise. I am a promise keeper. You both have been faithful. I am pleased with you both. Keep pursuing Me. I am pursuing you.

I love to hear Father's words. He cuts right to the heart and delivers a healing salve that only He can give. He knows just how to deal with our fears and lead us to truth. Fear masquerades in many forms, robbing us of the sheer delight of living fully alive. He is a liar and a deceiver. Unrestrained fear leads to unbelief. Unbelief is a lack of faith in God and reveals a heart that has not been made perfect in the love of God. If we know God, we know Love. And when we know Love, fear can't stand in His presence, so he flees. Perfect love casts out all fear.

Secret #6

Fear is dreaming with the devil. Know the Word of God so you can recognize the lies of the enemy.

Secret #7

Don't let your experiences, disappointments, or disillusions form your theology. Rather let the Word of God renew your mind with truth. God's Word trumps our experiences.

CHAPTER FIVE

You are What You Think:
Exposing the Obstacle of Unbelief

⚬❀⚬

Belief impacts the way we make choices and touches our experience,
while knowledge impacts our understanding. Knowledge changes what
we think. Belief changes the way we think.

~Ahab Alhindi, Limitless Intimacy

The journey started out like a honeymoon, but eventually reality would set in and a time of deeper trust would come. Because things hadn't happened in our timing and we didn't know how to walk this new Kingdom walk, fear turned into unbelief in areas. Unbelief is the second obstacle we need to remove from our lives. It will rob us blind of our destiny if we don't.

Fall Back

We left Oregon and came back across the country thinking our year of prep was done and now we were ready to receive our new ministry. God had given us a vision and a new dream. Nothing happened. We were expecting to have this amazing encounter with God, where most likely an angel would encounter us with his golden scepter and anoint us with the vision of all visions. Believe me, there are some strange things out there and that is not beyond the scope of imagination (especially mine), but most likely it would not happen in ways that I had expected. I did encounter an angel though. He sat on me at a conference we attended as a family back in 2010 on our way back from Oregon. I was laid out on the floor unable to move or talk for hours. In fact, the speaker had to step over me to get to the pulpit. During worship, I had an encounter with Jesus. We were dancing together to the song "Dance with Me" by Jesus Culture. Jesus was walking toward me on the stage and told me to fall back. Previously, my friend Ralph had sent me a text telling me that Jesus wanted me to fall back and I didn't have to understand. I just had to obey. It made no sense to me at the time, but in this moment, months later, Jesus stood before me and told me to fall back. I was crammed up against the front of the stage with people all around me packed in like sardines. I reasoned that if I fell back, I would be trampled to death. When I realized that I was arguing with Jesus and would probably end up losing, I just gave in and surrendered. I fell back and couldn't get up until hours later. I had no control whatsoever of my body. I couldn't walk, speak, or sit up. I was literally Jell-O. Troy had to carry me up to the hotel room and put me to bed. I didn't even brush my teeth that night; I was that incapacitated. Just sayin'. I don't know exactly the point of every encounter we have, especially when it comes to angels, but I do know they are sent to minister to us and carry out tasks on our behalf, as we speak out the will of God on earth. All I know is that I got up from the floor transformed by Love. I felt as though I had somehow come out of heart surgery and was empowered with the ability to trust more, because what was coming would rattle me to the core.

We wandered for a few years after that. I think we were disillusioned and naive. We read biographies of God using ordinary people to do extraordinary things in extraordinary ways. We had a cloud of witnesses, according to Hebrews 11, cheering us on, but no one to mentor us except from the pulpit of our church from a distance. There were also others that seemed to be on the same sort of "Joseph" journey: thrown into a pit, sold into slavery, moved up through the ranks, thrown in prison falsely and then promoted. It is humbling to think of Joseph's promotion. It is a heavy mantle to carry and I didn't want it until we were ready.

Doing Time in Texas

From NJ we ended up in Texas at a Jellystone Camping Resort. Troy was working for our campsite to live, making $7 an hour checking in campers, general maintenance of the campsites, and shoveling petting zoo poop, all while enduring people walking past telling their children, "See, that is why it is important for you to get an education, so you don't end up like that poor man." Troy has his Masters of Divinity degree, but that did nothing for him in our wilderness time. God was working. On the flip side, Troy had hours to sit and read and prepare for the vision that God had given us back in Oregon, while he was waiting to check the campers in. God uses everything. Texas was a difficult time for me mentally and emotionally. I remember walking the campground every night struggling to declare all the things I was grateful for because I had just found out I was pregnant. Surprise! I was living in a trailer, in the dead of summer, in Texas, and my husband was driving Yogi Bear around in a golf cart for a living. When the Holy Spirit led Jesus into the wilderness, He removed His presence from

Him experientially, not literally. Jesus was accustomed to talking to His Father and in the wilderness, He had to keep declaring, "it is written..." If Jesus could do it, so could I. So, I kept confessing His promises and His truth, even though I could not hear His voice and I did not understand. We give up the right to understand when we step out of the boat. You will need to get used to that.

Our time in Texas ended and we moved in with my brother-in-law in South Carolina so we could have the baby. Even during a financial drought, we were still bearing fruit, though not intentionally. It is an upside-down Kingdom. Before moving to Texas, we received a prophetic word that we would have two more boys. We would have a Brady Bunch, three boys and three girls. Nathan, baby number five, was born in my brother-in-law's house the day of his first date with his now wife Karen. I was in labor as he walked out the door and had Nathan in my arms when he came home. I had known we would be welcoming two more boys into our lives; I just didn't understand God's timing.

"We give up the right to understand when we step out of the boat."

All I Have to Give You is Jesus

God had promised us that there would be provision at the end of the journey. When that would be, we didn't know. There was not even a job prospect, although Troy had worked day and night sending out resumes, making calls, and studying to prepare for the vision God had given us. Had

God led us out into this wilderness to abandon us, pull the rug out from under us and strip us of all we had? No. He was, like Hosea 2:14 points out, *"luring us into the wilderness, to speak comfort to us."* Here, He would remove the shackles that kept us bound, so He could redefine our concept of relationship with Him and lead us in wisdom out onto the waters of His love. The beauty of the journey of faith is that you become more aware of your dependence on God and your beliefs become more solidified. You actually get a glimpse into what you really believe and who you really are. I remember a moment on the journey, after we had been stripped of everything, looking at Troy and through tears telling him, "All I have to give you is Jesus." I married a pastor, but I was not a pastor's wife anymore. I was a homemaker, without a home. We led no ministries, made very little money, had few possessions, and to many, we had no reputation. It was the most beautiful moment to realize that not many couples come to the place where they discover who they really are without anything to hide behind, and can actually say, "I am in love with you."

"All I have to give you is Jesus."

Preparing for a Curveball

In South Carolina, we were in the depths of our wilderness time. Finding a job was more difficult than we expected. Troy had been asked for his resume numerous times while he was an associate pastor, so we assumed it would be easy to find a job as a senior pastor when we were done "resting." WRONG! Troy practically had a full-time job searching for positions, writing resumes, and interviewing. The market was flooded with pastors and churches were closing left and right. The one-year gap on Troy's resume did not look good. It was almost as if God was blinding people to his resume or phone calls. Troy took whatever job he could get. He cleaned carpets, worked at a grocery store, and even helped a friend of ours, who was on a similar journey, do some masonry work up north. This kept him away for weeks at a time. After several years of this, we finally had a lead for a pastoring job in Connecticut. The process took an unheard of eight months. Troy was back and forth on the phone with the group of elders. We really loved them and desired to finally lead our own church, but the process was taking so long. All other doors seemed to shut before us, so all our eggs were in this one basket.

In my quiet time, God had told me to prepare for a curveball. That was a funny phrase that I never use, so it stuck out to me. In the middle of this candidating process, a pastor friend of ours, Chris Hussey from Abundant Life Community Church, called and invited Troy to come candidate at his church back in New Jersey, twenty-five minutes from our previous 10-year position. He was looking to hire a youth pastor. In our previous position, Troy was the pastor of adult ministries and had hoped to eventually become the senior pastor. Going back to New Jersey felt like it would be taking a step back, and yet, I longed to be with my friends back home in a life I loved. We were desperate and God knew we needed to be desperate to be teachable. Troy told Pastor Chris that we were in the process with another church, so Pastor Chris says out of the blue, "Well, if the Lord should send you a curveball, give me a call." There was our curveball. With that, we knew we were going back to New Jersey even though it didn't make sense. The candidate weekend with the Connecticut church came and went, along with the idea of pastoring our own church. God had been preparing us for a big vision. We weren't sure how that vision was going to play out, but it certainly didn't make sense that it would come about as a youth pastor. Here we believed God was preparing us in a different direction, but He was sending us back into ministry into a position that Troy was not even shaped for. God was up to something and I couldn't wait to see what He was going to do.

"Well, if the Lord should send you a curveball, give me a call."

Waiting for Breakthrough

We had been in South Carolina for almost four years waiting for the vision to happen. We waited somewhat patiently, and somewhat passively, because we didn't understand at that time how to use our words and our beliefs to confess that God *"gives life to the dead and calls those things which do not exist as though they did"* (Romans 4:17). We also had a fear of making the wrong decision and messing things up. We were piecing our theology together as we went and it wasn't always biblical. We made declarations, but they were not beliefs, just hopes. We were hanging on by a thread at times. God brought us beautiful people down South that were going through a similar "Joseph" journey. One afternoon our friends, Dominick and Natalie, were praying over us and Natalie had a strong word that our journey was not just about us, but what we were going through would give us the authority to release others from their bondage as well. God was building in us what was needed in order to carry the mantle He would place on our shoulders. That word sustained us and their friendship was a comfort to us. We were brought together by God during this time. Although we didn't know each other prior to South Carolina, we both had left successful careers in New Jersey and settled in South Carolina, with family, to have our babies. We also both moved back to New Jersey at the same time. I love how God works because it would have been a difficult time without our new friends.

Our debt had accumulated just trying to survive, so there was financial stress. My brother and sister-in-law needed to sell the house we were living in, rent free, because it was becoming a financial strain on the newlywed couple. We didn't want that for them. We didn't want this for us either, but we didn't know what else to do. Our pastor had counseled us and said he saw no sin in our lives and that we had such pure hearts and desire for the will of God. We were just pressing in for our breakthrough that never seemed to come. I don't even know what we were waiting for. I felt lost at this point. We were disappointed, disillusioned, and apart from a few friends and family that stood by us…totally alone. My friend Kristen Stoll later defined breakthrough as the following:

> If you wait for your breakthrough, you will be waiting your whole lifetime. This is your breakthrough. You are walking in it. Every revelation you have is your breakthrough…glory to glory. You are not waiting for your breakthrough. Now is the time to step out of the boat and walk on His Word. Embrace wisdom and hearken unto the voice of the Holy Spirit.
>
> Ask Father, 'What is the next step?
>
> …what is the next step?
>
> …what is the next step?'

Breakthrough IS every step you take toward Him in faith. I wish I would have had this perspective back then.

Build Your House

It is hard, at times, to take those steps of faith, especially when they come packaged in trials and pain. Being stripped or pruned is part of the process because it is removing all that will get in the way of the glory and prevent you from bearing fruit. We wanted this stripping even though it hurt. I believe the most difficult part of the journey for me was surrounding Micah's birth. Micah is our sixth child and another big surprise. He was on his way at the least opportune time of the journey. Micah was my "hairpin turn" and my "you've got to be kidding me." I have no idea how he was conceived because we had done everything, including nothing, to prevent pregnancy. All I know was that God wanted him interjected on the timeline of history on August 1, 2015. This period of time was probably the lowest part of the journey. Not Micah, but God's timing. I am totally in love with that boy, but pregnancy and birth and all that go with it, during such a tumultuous time, is another story. I remember sitting with the pregnancy test in my hand because I had skipped a period. I literally felt like I wanted to die. How could I tell people? People were worried enough for us, and now this. My mind went into the toilet and I thought of every reason this was not a good idea. I became hopeless, and I am not a hopeless person. I could feel the stress in my body. Why God? Why now? I carried all the responsibility and shame on myself.

He then interrupted my private pity party and asked me how my thoughts were working for me. I replied that they weren't doing so well. He gave me a tool that has changed my life. He spoke very firmly, "Build your house." He gave me Proverbs 24:3,4 which says, *"By wisdom a house is built, and through understanding it is established; through knowledge its rooms are filled with rare and beautiful treasures."* He continued to probe my heart to get to the real issues. "What kind of foundation are you building in your thoughts for understanding and knowledge to make their residency?" I responded that my wisdom or beliefs were that another child would be a financial burden. In my eyes, we were already struggling to care for what we had. I was too old, tired and worn out. We were a laughing stock and an embarrassment already. Because of these beliefs, my understanding was that we would have no money to care for our family. We would be homeless and destitute. As a result, my knowledge was hopelessness, fear, and unbelief. It was not a pretty picture nor was it a house I wanted to live in.

I realized I had partnered with the enemy's lies and agreed with them. God continued, "What is My wisdom? What understanding is established as a result? What are the treasures that fill each room when your foundation is secure in My truth?" I thought about it. I began to quote Scripture truths. *"Behold, children are a heritage from the LORD, the fruit of the womb is a reward. Like arrows in the hand of a warrior, so are the children of one's youth. Happy is the man who has his quiver full of them; they shall not be ashamed, but shall speak with their enemies in the gate."* Psalm 127:3-5. *"He who began a good work in you will bring it to completion at the day of the Lord Jesus Christ,"* Philippians 1:6. There were more, but I think you get the picture.

The more truth I spoke over my life, the more hope filled me and I was actually disappointed when the pregnancy test came back negative. His truth had so transformed my beliefs, that my understanding became clear that we would be taken care of. The next month the pregnancy test actually was positive. I was pregnant during my meltdown; it was just too soon to register and God knew I needed that time to build my house and prepare my heart for what was coming. We had never been without food or shelter. He had provided for us all the way, even if it didn't look like what we thought it was supposed to. When we are enslaved to wrong beliefs, we live from the posture of "not enough." During the wilderness season, we may survive with "just enough". But when we step out into our Promised Land, we will live from a posture of "more than enough", because like 2 Corinthians 9:8 states, *"God is able to make **all** grace **abound** toward you, that you, **always** having **all sufficiency** in **all** things, may have an **abundance** for **every** good work."* We will have plowed through the process in order to carry the destiny He has called us to carry, and in that process discover that His Word is true and He can be trusted because we do have a destiny in which we will thrive.

> *"By wisdom a house is built, and through understanding it is established; through knowledge its rooms are filled with rare and beautiful treasures."*

Micah's Birth

At the Connecticut church, where we had candidated, an elder's wife had prophesied into me that I was a bringer of life and the enemy couldn't believe I was still smiling. Here I thought I had been a disappointment to God because I had lost hope at times, but God was telling me that the enemy gave me his worst and I kept getting back up. I may have still been smiling, but my body was worn out with shame, worry, and anxiety. Shame, worry and anxiety is worship of the enemy and a sheer sign that you are believing lies about God. I didn't know my heavenly Father as Provider. The lies I had believed about Him in the area of finances almost cost me my life. If I could go back and live the journey all over again, (Oh please God, I hope we never have to) I would live it differently, because I believe differently. But at this point in time, my experience, disillusionment, and disappointment had created my theology, and I had believed somehow, I had failed God financially and I would have to work my way out of this hole. The hopelessness stemmed from not knowing how to do that. I still walked in performance, which is all about self. Later I would learn how to partner with God financially by believing differently, but we were still in the depths of process and didn't know where to go for answers.

A few months later, after dealing with all of the stress of almost being homeless, jobless, and penniless, I nearly died during childbirth because of my adrenaline and cortisol levels. Instead of oxytocin being released after birth; my body was flung into a state of an adrenaline surge, as if I was fighting a giant. And I was fighting a giant…the giant unbelief. Micah was born with the cord around his neck several times and had to receive CPR to resuscitate. As soon as the cord was cut, my body went into shock and convulsions. I could literally feel my body leaving and at that moment I wanted to go. I remember thinking, "I could just go and it will all be over." I seriously entertained this thought and knew I had a choice. But then I looked at Troy, holding the baby in his arms, with absolute panic on his face. I looked at Micah's little hands and feet and knew he would need a mother to love and nurture him. I couldn't stand the thought of him not knowing his mommy. And Troy, when the vision finally did happen, how would he possibly do it alone, without his butterfly? How could he bear this load and care for the needs of six children? I made the decision to stay and fight and believe. If this were a movie, the inspirational music would be playing in the background and the scene would move in slow motion. That is how I see it in my mind. It was a literal battle and the enemy could not believe I was still smiling. Micah's birth and my resolve to believe was a blow to his kingdom. The enemy doesn't understand love, especially a mother's love, because he is an orphan.

"And I was fighting a giant... the giant unbelief."

Making Mental Agreements with Truth

Throughout all of this, God was good. The enemy was doing his best to get us to believe otherwise. The facts were that life was falling apart all around us, but the truth from God's Word and the words prophesied over our lives were all we could keep confessing. According to Psalm 13:12, *"Hope deferred makes the heart sick, but a longing fulfilled is a tree of life."* Our hearts were sick, but we were pressing in for our breakthrough. **Many people simply have mental agreements with truth, rather than actual beliefs.** For example, I believed God is good because I read it in Scripture and have experienced His goodness in life in other areas. When life is good, well, of course God is good. But beliefs can be tested and challenged. Only until you walk through the fire does a truth become a belief in your heart rather than a belief in just your mind. Many people refer to this as the eighteen inches from head to heart. The heart and mind can have two different belief systems when we are out of alignment with God. When the funds ran out and Troy could not find a job, and people began to accuse him of being worse than an infidel because we were going deeper into debt, was God still good? When it seemed we were sinking rather than stepping into the words that God had given us or had been prophesied over us all across the country by many, was God still good? When friends and family turned on us and it seemed God was silent, was God still good? Absolutely.

Problems are Just Invitations to Solutions

Many turn their back on God when life doesn't make sense or it doesn't look the way we think it should. We blame God, instead of seeing problems as invitations to solutions as well as an invitation to know Him more. We are promised in God's Word that He came to give us life and life more abundant (John 10:10). Any time we are not walking in abundant life, joy, victory, success, or peace, the problem is not with God, it is with our belief systems. We are the negligible party here. He is perfect, absolutely dependable, and present to lead us into truth. And we are living proof that you can have joy and the abundant life even when life is falling apart all around you. Those things are not dependent on our situations or experiences. We possess them internally and can live from them in any storm. That is what Paul referred to when he said in Philippians 4:11-13:

> Not that I speak in regard to need, for I have learned in whatever state I am, to be content: I know how to be abased, and I know how to abound. Everywhere and in all things, I have learned both to be full and to be hungry, both to abound and to suffer need. I can do all things through Christ who strengthens me.

The enemy comes to steal, kill, and destroy. We live in a fallen world and bad things happen, even to good people. But God is still good and that does not change. He promises in Romans 8:28, *"All things work together for good to those who love God, to those who are the called according to His purpose."* We can't blame God when bad things happen and yet take credit ourselves when things are sunny. He is Lord over it all. Many times, we are not in control of what happens, but **we are always in control of how we respond. The outcome is determined by our response. Our response is determined by our character. Our character is formed under fire.** Like clay in the Potter's hand, He can make a masterpiece so long as the clay remains moldable.

Laughter is the Best Medicine

It is so important on the journey of faith to surround yourself with people of faith who will be there to speak life and encouragement to you, and if all else fails…make you laugh! I don't know what I would do without my friend Kelli. She is always good for a laugh to cheer me up and give me perspective. Her warfare is her laughter and when I get a snort, I am reminded that life is better when you can laugh at yourself. She is rarely good for a pity party and that is probably why she is the one I want to talk to when I feel like I am heading toward one. She reminds me that God gave me a sense of humor and I love to laugh too much to be in a pit, even if all eyes are on me and life seems to be falling apart all around me. God laughs at His enemies. See Psalm 37:13 and Psalm 2:4.

I laugh often now, when the enemy throws something at me, because I know he only has the power I give him, and he only wants to get me distracted from my destiny by speaking the opposite of what is true. Laughter is a powerful response. Thank God for children who naturally know how to laugh and bring a fresh perspective and relief at just the right time. Laughing is not only beneficial to your body, but it is just so fun to do. One afternoon my parents and my family were out for a picnic. My parents had my three-year-old Shanna in their car and we had the baby, Abby, in ours. Abby was giggling and we couldn't figure out what she was laughing at. She was just so amused by something. When we got to the park, my parents commented on how Shanna had been laughing hysterically in their car. They asked her what was so funny and she said, "Abby is so funny. She makes me laugh." Now mind you, they were in two separate cars, yet laughing simultaneously. We all looked at each other in amazement. That was totally outside the box, but hey, we are more spirit than flesh and I am not going to tell God what He can and cannot do. The Bible says in Psalm 135:6, "*Whatever the Lord pleases He does, in heaven and in earth, in the seas and in all deep places.*" Who's to say they were not doing battle in the heavenlies for us? Abby's name means "Source of the Father's Joy." Shanna's name means "Beautiful One of Light." Abby was birthed right before we left on this crazy adventure. God knew what we would need. She brought joy to our lives at a time when we were desperate for it. The encounter that day brought joy to us all, as well as a beautiful light of revelation, not to mention a great conversation that stretched our religious paradigm.

Building with Our Words

We also have ministering spirits that directly respond to God's truth when they hear it come from our mouths. It is as if they see light flash from our lips when we speak out God's truth and they are commissioned to fight on our behalf. Just as we have angels, there are also fallen angels, called demons, that are released to build strongholds through the lies that we speak. They are drawn to darkness. Proverbs 18:21 teaches that "*Death and*

life are in the power of the tongue, and those who love it will eat of its fruit."
The Kingdom of heaven is voice activated. Luke 6:45 says, "*A good man out of the good treasure of his heart brings forth good; and an evil man out of the evil treasure of his heart brings forth evil. For out of the abundance of the heart his mouth speaks.*" We are building our lives in the same way that God created heaven and earth by speaking words. If our words flow out of our heart, then it is important to make sure the heart believes truth.

"The Kingdom of heaven is voice activated."

Glistening Hope

Francis Frangipane said in his book *The Three Battlegrounds*, "Every area of your thinking that glistens with hope in God is an area which is being liberated by Christ. But any system of thinking that does not have hope, which feels hopeless, is a stronghold which must be pulled down." We are to constantly live in the expectancy that God's promises are "yes" and "amen," and we can hope for a desired outcome and expected end. In fact, I use this quote often to evaluate my life. If I am not particularly glistening with hope and am walking in impatience, doubt, or fear, I only have to stop and ask my Heavenly Father what is going on in my heart. I find that when He reveals His perspective and I come into agreement with the truth, the oppression lifts and my heart glistens again. It's also important here to interject that if we are not experiencing glistening hope because of a lie we believe, then we are in a sense choosing to live in mediocrity in this area of our lives.

Skidooing the Spirit of Offense

For example, one evening, my husband and I were walking down to the church for a date night, and I was running behind trying to get the children all settled. He decided to leave without me and meet me there because he doesn't like to be late. I had been looking forward to our date and getting away and resented his lack of acknowledging responsibility with helping settle the children. After all, why was it all on me? They were his children too. He could compartmentalize family life and responsibilities at work, but I was wrapped up in it all. I had a spirit of offense come upon me and whisper my rights. He was there to pat my back and agree with me on how selfish my husband had been. I was fuming mad by the time I walked down to the church...alone. I then realized who I had been partnering with. I pulled out a tool from my tool belt I had learned from an amazing book and workshop we had attended called *Love After Marriage* by Lori and Barry Burns. It was called the 1, 2, 3, Skidoo tool. I stopped and spoke out loud,

> I see you, offense. I see what you are trying to do. You pretend to be my friend, on my side, but you don't want my best. God will never play the accuser and accuse my husband, so you are a lying spirit sent to steal, kill, and destroy. You want to rob my children of their security by causing strife between their parents. You want to destroy my date night that I have been looking forward to, and you want to kill the connection between Troy and me. Well, I am not buying it. I am not partnering with you. I break agreement with the lies that I have declared and confessed out loud. Spirit of offense I send you away from me. I am created to walk in abundant life and I will only partner with God's truth.

I continued and asked Holy Spirit, "What do you want to exchange with me?" He answered that He wanted me to enjoy this night of connection with my man and He blessed me with peace. I received it and all of sudden the oppression left. I made the exchange. I partnered with God to bring heaven to earth. He is always there with the exchange. I literally felt lightness and walked off to enjoy the rest of my date. I realized that offense wasn't *my emotion*. It was a spirit and the spirit itself was feeling offense. I just took on his emotions as if they were mine.

It is important to know your normal so that when an abnormal emotion emerges, you can recognize it and deal with it. If offense is a normal emotion then that needs to be dealt with. Although it may be your normal, it is not normal in the Kingdom and not what God wants for you. Remember you walk in the abundant life. Glistening hope and joy should be every believer's norm. Offense, anger, bitterness, etc., are not your created personality traits. It is oppression from the enemy and needs to be sent away and replaced with truth and new habits.

Identity is the key to overcoming the obstacle of unbelief. Pure and simple, we need to believe what God says. Believing what God says is living by faith. Declare every day out loud, "I am who the Bible says I am. I have what the Bible says I have. I can do what the Bible says I can do." Knowing who we are and what our purpose is on earth will change everything. We are not just here to live out our days unto ourselves, instead we have the awesome privilege of bringing His Kingdom. Matthew 11:12 says, *"And from the days of John the Baptist until now the Kingdom of God suffers violence, and the violent take it by force."* We are not in a passive war. We take the Kingdom by force, but our warfare is not of this world. Write out scriptural promises and personalize them and declare them as your inheritance. I have included in the appendix some declarations/ confessions for you to declare and get you started. I encourage you to get your own rhema's from God's Word. These are specific words that God illuminates and breathes on from His written Word, the logos. Do this out loud every day until you believe it, and then keep doing it until the enemy believes you mean it.

> ## *"I am who the Bible says I am. I have what the Bible says I have. I can do what the Bible says I can do."*

Faith is a Person

Unbelief is a lack of belief or faith. Faith, according to Hebrews 11:1, *"is the substance of things hoped for, the evidence of things not seen."* Hope is a feeling of expectancy of a desired outcome and end. Hebrews says that faith is a substance, meaning it has a physical definition. I want to put before you that I believe faith is a person. If you continue with Hebrews 11, the Hall of Faith, you can see all that faith did through a person. We know that in Colossians 1:27 it says *"to whom God was pleased to make known what is the riches of the glory of this mystery among the Gentiles, which is Christ in you, the hope of glory."* I reason then that Christ in me is faith working in me, a person. I believe faith is the Holy Spirit. Back to Hebrews 11:

Now faith brings our hopes into reality and becomes the foundation needed to acquire the things we long for. It is all the evidence required to prove what is still unseen. This testimony of faith is what previous generations were commended for. Faith empowers us to see that the universe was created and beautifully coordinated by the power of God's words! He spoke and the invisible realm gave birth to all that is seen. Faith moved Abel to choose a more acceptable sacrifice to offer God than his brother Cain, and God declared him righteous because of his offering of faith. By his faith, Abel still speaks instruction to us today, even though he is long dead. Faith lifted Enoch from this life and he was taken up into heaven! He never had to experience death; he just disappeared from this world because God promoted him. For before he was translated to the heavenly realm his life had become a pleasure to God. And without faith living within us it would be impossible to please God. For we come to God in faith knowing that He is real and that He rewards the faith of those who give all their passion and strength into seeking him. Faith opened Noah's heart to receive revelation and warnings from God about what was coming, even things that had never been seen. But he stepped out in reverent obedience to God and built an ark that would save him and his family. By his faith the world was condemned, but Noah received God's gift of righteousness that comes by believing.

Faith moved Abel. Faith lifted Enoch. Faith opened Noah's heart to receive revelation and warnings from God. These people of faith were not moving on their own strength, but Christ in them, their only hope of glory. If faith is the person of the Holy Spirit, and allowing Him to live and move in and through us enables us to do glorious things, then it is important to get to know and believe the Holy Spirit. Unbelief is the opposite of having a relationship with Holy Spirit. Life with Him can be messy, but it is so glorious and so worth dismantling the obstacle of unbelief in order to attain it.

Powerful Peace

My daughter Ashley's name means a peaceful heart. She loves her name, but always felt embarrassed of the meaning of her name. In her mind, that meant weak and quiet and she is anything but weak and quiet. One day at a conference, Pastor Paul Martini gave the most profound definition I have ever heard of peace. He was speaking about how the Kingdom of heaven was not about eating and drinking, but righteousness, peace, and joy in the Holy Ghost (Romans 14:17). His definition of peace finally helped me understand the Kingdom. Righteousness, I understood. We are the righteousness of Christ. It is our identity. Joy was how we walked in the Kingdom. Joy is a state of inner gladness, contentment, delight or rejoicing. It is expressed from the inside out. It is the overflow of what has happened inside the reborn heart. Joy is independent of the surrounding environment and not based on favorable circumstances, but rather a spiritual reality, and a gift from God. If righteousness is who we are and joy is how we accomplish something, then peace is what we do. Peace is an action word. According to Pastor Paul (based on the original characters of the Hebrew word), "peace is destroying the authority attached to chaos." Isn't that powerful? It is active. It is warfare. It is anything but weak and quiet. I looked over at Ashley and asked her, "How do you like your name now?" She smiled from ear to ear. It was getting through. Knowing her name and her identity gave her power. Knowing who you are makes you confident and powerful. The more we know the Word of God and believe it, the more powerful we become in His Kingdom.

"...peace is destroying the authority attached to chaos."

I encourage you to get alone with God and let Him love on you. Journal and talk through Scripture with Him. Tell Him when something doesn't make sense. He is big enough to handle your questions, doubts, hurts, anger, and disappointments. I always feel better when I spend time with God and get His perspective. His perspective changes everything. When we spend time with Jesus, we learn He is everything but religious. We as humans like to box things in, but He enjoys opening the box and exposing what is inside so we can be free. He knows that when we don't know who we are, we strive and perform. Faith is Christ in me. Striving is me in me.

Happiness by a Lake

One evening we were traveling to life group, which was an hour away. We were in a rich prophetic environment and our life group had some amazing prayer warriors and well-seasoned ministers of the miraculous. We were drinking in all we could and received all God had to teach us. It was hard to receive all the time. I began to believe that because I was new in the prophetic that I didn't have much to offer because I didn't look like them. Words of knowledge and prophecy were still pretty foreign to me.

In fact, years before in our little basement church, one of the guys had an open vision. He was enabled to see everyone through heaven's eyes and what we were all doing in the Kingdom. My husband was building the foundation of the new Jerusalem. My friend Rana was keeping the flame burning by the throne. Everyone seemed to have these important jobs or "identities." I asked what I was doing and he said, "I see you walking with a smile by a lake." What? Come again? That's it? Go back. That can't be right. I don't want to be walking by a lake. I want to be building the Kingdom. I felt gypped because I only had my limited perspective of the vision. I hadn't asked God what He saw and why He placed me happy by a lake. He told me later that my job was to minister to Him. He just wanted to be with me. The lake was a reservoir of His joy, and the more I spent in His presence the more the reservoir would overflow to the people around me. They were thirsty for joy and just by being with Him, I was a dispenser of His presence. I liked who I was after that…happiness by a lake. That's me.

"Faith is Christ in me. Striving is me in me."

Lion Licked

So, fast forward to this night on the way to group, and here I am forgetting who I am and what I bring. I wanted desperately to be used by God by bringing a powerful word or prophecy. I wanted to look like someone else. I decided to ask God for something to give to these people that have loved us so richly. Now the following may stretch you. It stretched me. I am not religious anymore. Grounded in the Word, yes, but religious, no. I am not going to pretend I know all and have God all figured out. In fact, the more I learn, the more I realize there is to learn. When I close my eyes and allow Holy Spirit to use my imagination, I often meet Jesus and He appears to me in the form of a lion. Lions are strong and protective. I can run my fingers through His mane and even feel the oils on my hands. He came to me as a lion this night in the car on the way to group. I asked Him seriously to give me a word for someone. He just licked me. I asked again and He continued to lick me. I begged Him to stop and take me seriously. I began to laugh hysterically, still begging Him to stop. Troy was driving in the seat next to me unfazed. He was used to my strange and out-there relationship with God.

When we arrived, I was disappointed because God hadn't given me a word and I had nothing to bring except slobber. When we walked in the door, the group was already standing in a circle holding hands in prayer. The room felt heavy and serious. We quietly slipped in. I grabbed the person's hand on my left and immediately they fell down. I grabbed the person on the right and they did the same. They began to roll around laughing. All around me people were falling on the floor, rolling around laughing when minutes before the atmosphere was thick with heaviness. I was so naive, wondering what was happening. The leader looked up through her laughter and announced to me, "When you walked in, you were slathered in the glory!" I had been Lion-licked. I was slathered in the glory because I had been with Him. When I arrived, I had brought the joy of our relationship. My lack of knowing who I am in Christ, who He is to me, and what He wants to do in and through me, almost robbed me of the opportunity to minister in a totally unique way that only I can bring. We all have our own special identity. When we spend time with Jesus, and read and meditate on His words, we learn who we are and we fall in love with who He is. We can't be in His presence and remain the same. We are always changed from glory to glory. He told me I am happiness by a lake. I can either choose to believe that or walk by my feelings and believe a lie.

Just Be

In another instance, at the same church, I was on the prayer team. People came from all over the world to receive prayer at this church. That was a little intimidating, especially being around such well-seasoned prayer warriors. My time at All Nations Church really helped me develop the gifts I carried while teaching me not to compare myself, but rather discover how God wants to use me. I am a seer. I see in pictures and work best when ministering in a group. I was a little embarrassed of my gift, truthfully. I would see pictures when I prayed for people like an image of the Jolly Green Giant, or I would see Jesus throwing apples at someone. Sometimes I would just see a color and a word. These images completely wrecked the people they were directed towards, but to me they seemed silly and child-like. I had to learn to trust Papa to speak through me and that He knew better than I did what the person in front of me needed to hear.

This one particular morning at church, a lady approached our group for prayer. We were in groups of three up at the front of the church. The first person began to prophesy over her and speak with such elaboration and power. The second did the same. The woman began to tear up. I felt kind of embarrassed and silly with what I had. I began to tell the lady that what I saw was an apple tree laden with many apples. It was so full they were falling to the ground. Immediately she fell to the floor and started weeping and praising God. I looked around at the others on the prayer team completely surprised. When she finally stood up, she relayed that ten years prior she had seen a vision of an apple tree with no fruit. It was dried up and neglected; she was in such a dry place. The image Father had given me for her restored her hope and confirmed the direction she had been praying about for her life. It obviously touched her in deep places.

People come up to me, often years later, reminding me of a word I had spoken over them that touched their life and how God continued to expound and unpack it for them. A picture is worth a thousand words, especially if it is from God. Never disqualify your gift. Ask Him to give you things for others and He will faithfully do it, but it may come in a way you are not expecting. Just deliver what He gives you without elaboration or interpretation unless, of course, He provides. Remember it is God that is wanting to connect to the people in front of us and He speaks through us. We are not manufacturing the words, but positioning ourselves as a vessel for Him to move through. That takes the pressure off of you to perform. If it helps, lean into Him as if He is over your shoulder. Ask Him what He wants to say and then wait. The cool part about partnering with God and serving the person in front of you, is that you get to be an eyewitness to the truth that God pours out through you. A new revelation of the Father is revealed and you both get ministered to. **The kingdom is all about abundance and overflow; it's just God's nature.** God gives us gifts to equip the body and encourage others. When we embrace them and steward them, He can do amazing things through our lives. Rest in who He created you to be and in the gifts He has given. He will use you mightily in the Kingdom.

Our Warfare is Rest

Our greatest warfare is when we rest. Rest means to believe. Hebrews 4:10,11 states, "For he who has entered His rest has himself also ceased from his works as God did from His. Let us therefore be diligent to enter that rest, lest anyone fall according to the same example of disobedience." The only thing we are called to be diligent in is rest. Not works. The example Paul is referring to is when the Israelites wandered in the wilderness due to unbelief. Although Moses knew he was a son, the Israelites didn't want to see God face-to-face and instead wanted to receive secondhand what Moses received from God. Exodus 20:19 says; "Then they said to Moses, 'You speak with us, and we will hear; but let not God speak with us, lest we die.'" They wanted to remain comfortable in their ways. They didn't want to step out of the boat and risk losing themselves and their comforts. They did not know God; therefore, they did not know themselves. As a result, they kept grumbling and complaining, doubting God, and wandering. Their unbelief is what ultimately prevented them from entering the Promised Land. Unbelief is an insidious obstacle that robs you of God's best. He wants an intimate relationship with us, like He had with Moses. **Religion keeps us wandering in the wilderness, living off of someone else's relationship instead of entering into our own.** It is so important to know who God is so that you can know who you are. Without that, you will never see your true destiny.

Secret #8

Build your house - Proverbs 24:3-4

Secret #9

Know God and know your identity.

Secret #10

Rest is your greatest warfare.

Secret #11

Laughter is good medicine, so laugh at the enemy.

CHAPTER SIX

God's Not Dead...Religion is: Exposing the Obstacle of a Religious Mindset

The biggest enemy we face isn't the enemy; it's passivity, and a meek acceptance of the majesty of God. It's a gradual falling off of awe, a reluctant nod where a huge grin should be. The Good News becomes just okay news.

Christianity becomes life enhancing instead of life changing. We stop being radicals, because we think it's enough just to be 'nice.' A cup of coffee in the morning is 'nice.' It's 'nice' when we get nothing but green lights on the way to work. 'Nice' people only finish last because they're content not to be first, and when the Church becomes willing to settle for being 'nice,' the Church becomes dull, predictable and monotonous. We need to live in wonder and astonishment at the Kingdom we've inherited, not be blasé about it.

~**Graham Cooke**

In my quiet times, I often picture meeting Jesus somewhere so we can talk, just the two of us. It varies where we visit. I just rest my thoughts and go where my imagination takes me. It usually involves water. Most of the times we are by the sea, but on this particular day, as I spent time with Him, I had a vision that I was in the middle of a tranquil river that ran through the quietest mountain scene. Pine trees decorated the landscape and mountain cliffs towered overhead. A lazy river twisted around a bend and there sat the perfect fishing hole. The water was clear enough to drink as it drifted over smooth stones. The air had a fall chill and the sun was saying its goodbyes with hues of purple and orange. I stood in waders with water up to my lower thighs out in the middle of the waving current. Peaceful. Tranquil. Quiet. I met Jesus there. I didn't know why He wanted to meet there, although I liked it. The scene brought peace to an area in my heart I hadn't connected with in a while. There was Jesus in His waders, fishing basket and baseball cap. We stood quietly casting our lines in and out. Fly fishing relaxes me. I not only love to fly fish, but I love to watch others fly fish. It just calms me. As He cast His line out and in while we both stared out into the river, He asked me, "How many fish have you caught?" I looked into my fishing creel, which revealed that I was there more for the serenity than the fish and added, "Not much, how about you?" "Same," He responded.

I began to think in my mind that I should have had more fish. Maybe I was not trying hard enough. I started to lose my peace and I asked Him, "Why did you want to know?" He kind of smirked and answered, "Just wanted to know if you were having as bad a time catching fish as Me." I smiled, staring straight out at the river, not expecting that kind of answer from Jesus. He then turned His face toward mine and looked at me deep in the eyes and followed with, "I am not fishing this afternoon to catch fish. I just love to be with you." Jesus knew my tendency to perform for love and He knew just how to silence my performance with His love.

The third obstacle I want to shed light on is the obstacle of a religious mindset. It masquerades as legalism, performance, complacency, passivity, a poverty spirit, false humility (which is just another name for pride because the focus is still on self), or ignorance. It is established in wrong beliefs. Just as fear and unbelief need to be demolished through renewing our mind and believing differently, so too does a religious mindset.

"I am not fishing this afternoon to catch fish. I just love to be with you."

Eating from the Wrong Tree

This journey for me started years before we had our "Exodus." The journey was only the impetus that brought it all together. I say "Exodus," because when one is stuck in a religious mindset, they might as well be in a prison or a slave making bricks out of straw for Pharaoh. Some people have these amazing salvation moments and they celebrate their spiritual birthdays every year because their lives will never be the same. My journey began as a search for the "right" way to live life, as if there was one secret formula to discover what would lead to a life free of pain, sickness, sadness and disappointing God. Formulas are only steps we search out to try and gain some sort of control over our lives that promise comfort and an easy life;

like a magic pill or step-by-step process you can follow with your eyes closed. Life is neither a formula nor a set of legalistic rules. And if it is to you, most likely you have bought into a religious mindset. I ended up eating from the wrong tree in the garden – the Tree of the Knowledge of Good and Evil. The enemy knows that if he can get people to eat from the only tree God told us not to eat from, then he can distort the truth and bring deception. He can undermine what God has spoken and redefine good and evil. He can get us focused on the natural realm, as well as on ourselves, and trick us into believing God is *withholding* something from us instead of *protecting* us. When we partake of the fruit from this tree, our gaze turns inward, we see our nakedness and shame, and we live according to our own covering...self-righteousness. Eating from this tree causes a spiritual death because it makes us judges of good and evil. We no longer trust and abide, but rather strive and wonder, because the buck stops with us.

Satan was crafty. He deceived Adam and Eve in the beginning because he wanted their earthly throne. He wanted to rule and reign like God. In the garden account found in Genesis chapter 3, Satan knew just how to deceive Eve and steal away her inheritance. He got her to doubt God's nature and believe He was withholding something from her. He undermined her identity by telling her that when her eyes were opened, she would be like God. What she didn't realize was that she was already like God. She was perfect and created in His image, and yet, the enemy deceived her into believing that her identity was not complete. The ability to judge good and evil apart from God would somehow make her enlightened, but it only led to shame and separation. She could no longer see herself the way God saw her. She had a lie that tainted her view of herself and others. That is what many suffer from when they don't know who God created them to be. They only know what they have become.

"...when one is stuck in a religious mindset, they might as well be in a prison or a slave making bricks out of straw for Pharaoh."

The Bondage of Legalism and Self-Righteousness

Life as a Christian was all about discipline and dying to myself. Well, dying to myself is what I did, but it was not the dying God desires. Jesus came to give a deathblow to the sin nature so that we can live life from His presence where there is fullness of joy. He came to fulfill the old covenant and initiate a new one through the cross and resurrection (Matthew 5:17). I had faith in God, but my beliefs were all wrong. I had "self" righteousness, which by definition is striving to attain my own righteousness. I didn't know that through Christ I was already made righteous. There was nothing I could do to add to or take that away. I was made complete through Christ. My heart and mind just needed to get the memo.

As a newly married woman, I felt ill-equipped on what it meant to be a wife, and then a few years later, a mother. I felt that everything about me was frivolous and wrong. I desperately wanted to be a good wife and mother and didn't know how to do it without making a mistake. I was listening to all the voices around me telling me what was expected of me as a pastor's wife, and the gamut of books I read sent conflicting messages about what it looked like to be a godly wife or mother. I never felt I was good enough for God. He seemed to have these unreachable standards that no matter how much I died to myself, I could never seem to hit the mark. I always felt inadequate. I didn't know how to have a relationship with God, so in fear, I resorted to hiding behind rules hoping to cover all my bases. They weren't God's rules. They were mine. Religion seeks to create rules instead of walk in a relationship because it is more controlled.

I looked around at what I thought a Christian was supposed to look like and I tried to conform. I cleared my home of all the "bad" influences I could think of. Instead of asking Holy Spirit which influences needed to be removed, I lumped it all together and threw it all out. I guess I thought I would be earning brownie points with God, as if He would look down and declare us righteous because of something we had done. Legalism had me by the throat and religion had sucked the life out of living. I resented salvation, as I understood it, and I resented marriage even more. Neither were the gifts the Bible had spoken about. They both were burdens I couldn't carry. When you spend your life trying to figure out what God's will is, so that you don't make a mistake, or so that you can do the "right" thing, then God seems cruel and evasive. Why would He make me this way only to ask me to die to it? I couldn't push the beautiful frivolities God had placed inside of me down deep enough. They kept manifesting. "Unsanctified", so I thought, dreams kept surfacing. Love and joy kept calling to me, but I believed I had to die to my life so that I could find it and to me that meant dying to anything that I thought was not "spiritual." Why would

He make me love beauty and be filled with such passion only to tell me to crucify it and hate this world? The messages were so confusing.

I would say often, "I would be a better person if I were not a Christian." In fact, this very reason was why I never wanted to share my faith with anyone. I could see what I had to offer someone down in the dumps, because their life couldn't get any worse. At least they could look forward to heaven. To someone living what seemed a "good life," what did my "gospel" have to offer? It wasn't a gift. It was a death sentence in this life even if it meant eternal life with God. And why wouldn't God just take us to heaven after we were saved if life on earth was just to be a living hell? So many questions, and in time, God would help me find the answers. Eventually, I would find Him and shed this shell of religion that looked good on the outside, but on the inside was just dead man's bones.

Performing for Love

My pride had blinded me to the truth. It all came down to free will and performance. Jesus willingly laid His life down. It wasn't taken from Him. By trying to do the right thing all the time, I was a prisoner to a standard I could never attain. I wasn't laying my life down in submission. I was performing for love and acceptance and my heart was far from God. It was on myself. I had no idea what the true gospel was about. It isn't about self-preservation, but redemption. It's not about what we can do, but about what He already did. Jesus came to redeem us, to restore us back to our original design. He came to do what we could never do and be for us what we could never be. I didn't have to perform anymore. I was already accepted. Now I could walk out the destiny He had created for me to walk in without fear of making a mistake. I wasn't working for an inheritance. I had one. All it took was believing it was mine. Ephesians 2:8-9, *"For by grace you have been saved through faith, and that not of yourselves; it is a gift of God, not of works, lest anyone should boast."* His abundant grace, plus my believing faith in what He has already done, is the simple gospel. I had attached a pharisaical list of laws to my faith and tried to add to what Jesus had done as if His righteousness wasn't enough. I had to add mine, which the Bible calls filthy rags (Isaiah 64:6). How arrogant. Through my performance, I chained myself to a standard I set for myself that robbed me of my free will to choose life. We need not make rules about "gray" areas such as media choices, alcohol, or clothing style. Instead, we need to walk in relationship with God and allow Him to lead us in each decision. I had no hope because I thought I had salvation, but no free will, and that is no life at all. It's not even biblical.

When you live from legalism, it is an endless pit of rules that lead you further and further away from Truth. Each person has their own walk with God and we should not impose our rules as law onto others when God didn't even do that. He summed up His laws in two statements: love God and love others (Matthew 22:36-40). He knew if we would fulfill these two, then we would fulfill all the others as well. Living under the law, or under the old covenant, creates rules and boxes our relationship with God into a list of do's and don'ts. The focus is on performance. Grace opens you up to a relationship and a conversation. I have since learned to ask myself if what I am about to watch, listen to, wear, do, or say will bring me closer in my relationship to God and others or put distance between us. My decisions are not based in fear, but love. God enjoys being a part of all my decisions now. Not as a tyrant, but rather, a friend. Renewing your mindset is a process. Salvation is an experience. Faith takes time. God is patient in the process with us.

A Man-Centered Gospel

I remember early on in my walk, sitting out on my back deck and God asked me, "If your husband left and your children walked away from the faith, would you still follow me?" I answered honestly, "No." At that point, I came to Jesus because I thought He would make me a better person and help me get the family I always wanted. The Bible's principles work for anyone, saved or unsaved. There are spiritual laws that govern our lives, like physical laws such as gravity, and believe them or not, they are true. Many millionaires have built their empires on the foundation of Scripture's spiritual laws, sometimes unknowingly, because the truth had just been repackaged with different words from a different source. That said, coming to Jesus because He will improve your life is the wrong motivation. Unfortunately, that is how many false converts are created. Life enhancement is not the true gospel. The focus is on self and building your own kingdom. God wants our lives to be successful, and because He created us, He knows how best we thrive. Left to ourselves we become slaves to whatever we focus on. We are designed to worship something. I would rather worship the One who is perfect, just, and loving. But that was not the God I knew or had been taught about. My god was temperamental, never satisfied with my best, and loved me only if I performed perfectly. Later I would learn that I had just transferred my "beliefs" about how I felt my earthly family felt toward me onto God. This healing process with my earthly family God would also redeem as we stepped out. He takes good care of His children and loves them back to wholeness.

I "came" to Jesus originally because I didn't want to go to hell and that seemed like a no-brainer. I was never discipled though. I just started serving and working at not disappointing God. That is what I believed He wanted. God's standards became exhausting. Our beliefs about God affect everything, and I did not know God. I only knew what I experienced through my filter of half-truths. I took on a morality because it was the "right" thing to do and because God was up there with His list of "what not to do", now that I was a "believer." But I wasn't a believer really. I just believed in God, but I did not know Him nor His words or ways. Demons believe in God and they tremble, but that doesn't make them saved (James 2:19). I thought God was a cosmic killjoy, but I was told heaven would be worth it.

The longer I lived, the more I wondered if it really was worth dying to everything I loved to be a moral person for the assurance of an afterlife. And is it really much of a morality if you are forced to have it? How much of a relationship can you have with someone who has a gun to your head? What kind of a relationship can you have with someone you are afraid of? It is also hard to grasp the concept of tomorrow and laying down the immediate gratification for the hopes of a better afterlife. But you see, I had it all wrong, and I had it all wrong for a long time. I was good at performing. I was good at doing the right thing in hopes that it would get me love. That's ultimately what I really wanted...love. But I secretly resented the very God I thought was supposed to love me.

Troy is Coming

Consequently, I spent my teenage years searching for love. I had lived with the bitter taste of rejection my whole life and thought if I could just be good enough, I would be chosen. I had my heart broken a few times and broke a few hearts a few times too. So, when it came time to marry, I didn't feel competent to make the right choice. I had a skewed understanding of the sovereignty of God, so I surrendered to Him and declared, "Obviously I don't know how to do this thing called love. I need you to choose for me." Troy had unknowingly traveled all across the country to find his bride, who wasn't exactly waiting for him. He was in seminary and on his one-year internship out in California where I was the church secretary and part-time student at the local junior college. I was floundering in life and desperately trying to find myself when God met me in the balcony of my little church while I was setting up for the service for the upcoming weekend. The lights were out, with only the faint rays of sun reaching in from the windows out in the foyer. It was then that I heard an audible voice, "Troy is coming."

I jerked around to see who was in the room, but no one was there. "Troy is coming?" Immediately, in my heart, I remembered in seventh grade telling God that I wanted to marry a Troy. I also remembered that God had told me I was going to be a pastor's wife when I was in tenth grade. I had been sitting in the back of the church with all the other teenagers, most only there for the social experience and because it was what you were supposed to do on a Sunday morning. In the middle of the service I noticed the pastor's wife appearing to attentively listen to her husband preach a message she had probably heard many times before, but all the same, she sat with a smile on her face staring in his direction even if her thoughts may have been a million miles away. I had never really noticed her before, but I sat transfixed by the idea of what her life must be like. In the middle of my observance a voice broke into my thoughts, "That is you."

Assuming the voice to be God, I adamantly responded almost out loud, "Oh no, I don't play the piano, and I don't teach Sunday School, and I CERTAINLY don't want to be a poor man's wife. You don't know me at all."

The interchange freaked me out a bit. All I knew was that I wanted to marry a man with money and live far away from here, somewhere close to New York City. I had seen the city many times on the big screen and had romanticized the idea of living a life like in the movies: a life completely different than my own. Sometimes our dreams are just reactions to our past disappointments and experiences. I didn't know a Troy nor was I ready for such news. I had my life planned out and Troy, whoever he was, was not in the picture.

The next day, centered on the green felt bulletin board, was a picture of a Midwestern boy, desperately trapped in the eighties. He had a buttoned-down shirt, double paned glasses and hair parted down the middle. Underneath his picture, in bold-faced print, were the words "Pastoral Intern, Troy Bramblet." I thought to myself, "That's my husband? No, it couldn't be." I had been dating my high school sweetheart for six years waiting around for him to decide to grow up and marry me. He was enjoying his youth in southern California while I waited up north for the big question…which never came. This Troy embodied the exact opposite of everything I had pursued my entire life, and yet, upon meeting him, my heart felt strangely at home and at peace with a guy that instantly became my best friend. He only needed a bit of tweaking and a shopping spree, but even that could not fix the fact that he was in school to be a pastor, and to me, that meant he would be poor.

After fighting it for a year, a few months before he was set to go back to school in New York, I decided I would be losing my best friend and suggested that he take me with him. He had fallen in love with me months earlier, but I had been suffering from a bitter broken heart from my previous relationship. In spite of the insanity of a quick romance, we were married two months later. I didn't want to wait around any longer while other people lived their dreams, leaving me stuck and lonely. Troy was my best friend, but nonetheless, we were not prepared for what was to come. For this couple, our life would begin not in marital bliss, but in the trenches of tough love.

The Fruit of Passivity

I had no idea the repercussions of understanding free will and laying down performance would have on my relationships. I had believed becoming a pastor's wife and spending my life in ministry would be doing the "right" thing and God would be pleased and choose me, because up until that point, I had lived my life for myself and it had brought me nothing but pain. I have always loved my husband, but I knew part of my heart was far away from him because I hadn't felt marrying him was my choice. He was my best friend, but I had closed my heart off to him as my lover, because a lover had the power to hurt me and I never wanted to feel the pain of rejection again. The sad truth of closing your heart off for fear of rejection, is that you also close it off to love and the many adventures love brings with it along the way. In my mind, I believed God had brought me a best friend that would never hurt me, but He was bringing me a lover that would draw my heart out to trust. I had believed for so long that God had chosen for me, without my free will. This is the result of the wonderful fruit of passivity we as Christians often eat and label it, God's sovereignty. Is He sovereign? Yes. Does He want us to use that as an excuse to live passive lives in fear of making wrong choices or to explain away when something doesn't go how we thought it should? No. I had given up my free will and laid it on the altar of religion. As I have grown in faith, and in love with my heavenly Father, I have come to realize the gift He brought me in my husband. He knew way before me what my heart needed, but because I had decided I had no choice, my marriage became what God originally knew our relationship with Him would be like if He did not give us free will…like puppets. When I realized that Troy was exactly whom I would have chosen had I felt I could choose, all of a sudden, my heart was restored and I began to dream again. The passion surfaced and my heart was set free. So many of our marriages reflect what is going on in our relationship with God and vice versa. They are mirrors of each other. Because of the truths I have been learning and the new relationship with my Savior I have been walking in, I am now so in love with my husband after twenty-two years of marriage. I not only have a best friend, but also a lover, and that combination is the most fulfilling marriage one can experience. I feel like I am on my honeymoon and I feel the same way with God.

Coming Out of the Dark: Why Didn't I Have Free Will?

Now, I am not saying that life was all bad or that I didn't have a relationship with God at all. On our journey, He was leading me into the truth of who He is and I was confronting every "truth" I had ever been taught or believed. I was coming out of Egypt into my Promised Land. I was beginning to see that faith is a journey we take with Jesus, not a destination. One particular afternoon, I sat in a parking lot alone after watching a matinee movie. I was wrecked because, through the movie, my questions came to a head and I couldn't push myself down any longer. I was losing my way and there had to be more to this "faith-walk" than what I was living. In the movie, the family, who were not believers, had this beautiful life of laughter and togetherness. They were all pursuing their passions freely and nothing was holding them back from achieving their dreams. There was no one telling them their dreams were wrong or that they should be doing this or that. I just noticed they had free will. Why didn't I? I saw God in everything. I could see His diversity, beauty, love, and joy, and yet somehow, I separated the two. There was God, and then there was my belief and theology (the beliefs I actually lived out subconsciously). My beliefs, and the God I served, didn't seem to line up with the God of Scripture. I was just following religion, not God, and religion seemed to have everyone in a box with its man-made formulas and cookie cutter conformity. Religion seemed irrelevant to me for life, but I was curious about this God I was learning about.

Through reading the Bible and attending a Spirit-filled church, I was beginning to see who God really was and who I was to Him. He had given me signs all my life, but I saw them through a religious filter. You see, the simple perspectives that I was beginning to learn on our journey were the difference between me and my unsaved neighbor. I had no idea what my salvation cost my Savior. I had no idea what it truly meant to be saved. I knew what I was saved from, but not what I was saved to. I didn't know my purpose for life here on earth now that I was saved. I knew nothing about the Kingdom of God.

"I knew what I was saved from, but not what I was saved to."

The Real Good News, The Gospel of the Kingdom

As sons and daughters of the King of kings, we build His Kingdom on earth as it is in heaven. I knew the gospel in relation to sin, but not the gospel of the Kingdom (Matthew 24:14). I was missing an important part...a relationship with Jesus, the King, and the expansion of His Kingdom. I had known I had a Savior, but I didn't know I had a King and that this King had a Kingdom. He came to set His children free to rule and reign in that Kingdom...not just when we die, but now. That family in the movie I saw that afternoon made me jealous of their free will. I began to ask myself what did I have that they didn't? What about the gospel was good news because to me it never seemed like good news unless I was dead? That family in the movie may have had free will, but were they really free? On the outside they may laugh and play together, they may pursue their passions at will, but where is their hope? They were dead in their sin, but they seemed to have more joy and peace in this life than I had. Sure, I had eternal life, but I knew my life did not look attractive to unbelievers. Truthfully, we were both bound by an old nature. The only difference was I had been redeemed from mine, but not living it, and they didn't know there was a Redeemer to set them free. We lived no differently in our lives—both of us were prisoners of performance, a product of the fall, and a slave to self-preservation. They at least were able to pursue their dreams and passions. This world is as good as they will ever know, and my life felt like a living hell because I didn't understand redemption, my identity, my inheritance, and the power of my beliefs. I was a believer who didn't believe. I believed some things, but I didn't believe the whole picture. I believed through a religious filter…a religious mindset. I wanted a free will. I didn't want a free will to go and sin. I wanted to be free. I wanted to laugh and dream, and the freedom to stretch beyond my limitations.

I was finally asking God the real questions I had. I wanted to know if it was okay to be me. Just me. Not what I was supposed to be. Not what I thought a good Christian looked like. I wanted to know what He saw when He looked at me. If He only saw Jesus when He looked at me then what was the point of me? I had died to an old sin nature, but what did the resurrected new nature look like? I wanted to leave my old nature at the cross and step into the resurrection and keep walking. I wanted to walk on water. I didn't want to keep focused on death, but learn what it meant to be fully alive. If Jesus came to give us abundant life, then what did that life look like? I wanted to know what I was saved to. I had so many questions and now that I finally gave myself permission to ask my real questions, I could start having the conversations God had been waiting for us to have. This book is the answer to those questions. We all were on our own personal journeys, but this was mine. He took me on a journey into my heart and uprooted the lies that didn't belong; those lies that were preventing me from stepping into my created destiny.

The true gospel is receiving Jesus because He is the only way to be reconciled to God. Our sin has left a vast debt and only Jesus provided the perfect, sinless sacrifice that pays our debt. Apart from Jesus we can do nothing to save ourselves. We are justified by putting our faith in the person of Jesus to save us and cleanse us of all our unrighteousness. Then we are born again and we get to exchange our old nature for a new one. Jesus didn't come to polish up our old nature. He came to kill it, on the cross, with Him. He became sin and everything attached to it: curses, sickness, disease, poverty, lack, the iniquities of past generations and anything else the enemy had perverted. God's wrath toward sin was poured out on Jesus and the debt was finally paid once and for all. Jesus looked the enemy in the face and told him, "What you have done to my child through sin, I now take upon Myself and exchange it for My perfection. They no longer resemble what sin has distorted. You had your time in their life, but now they are perfectly clean and they wear My robes and carry My authority. All that is Mine, I give to them." He came to resurrect His perfect nature in us so that we could live lives of righteousness, peace, and joy in the Holy Spirit. We could become the best versions of ourselves, made complete in Jesus. We were created in the image of God, and through Christ, He restored us to that perfect image He originally created in the garden. What was marred through sin was now restored. **When God looks at us, He sees Jesus expressed through our unique personalities.** He loves my frivolous and beautiful nature, because I was created in His image. He didn't want my personality to die, He wanted my sin nature to die so that I could step into my original design in Christ. We become the righteousness of Christ and that is what God sees when He looks at us. He sees the image of His perfect Son packaged in our personality. He sees us as the best version of ourselves…completely redeemed. All things are made new. We have new hearts and new desires. We spend the rest of our lives discovering what our inheritance is as believers.

Dreaming with God

Understanding my new nature and the truth of the gospel of the Kingdom, as well as the significance of the New Covenant versus the Old, was opening my eyes to what my heart had been longing for. The gospel IS good news. I just had so much to "unlearn". I had viewed God through a religious lens my entire life and completely missed His true nature. What I had been taught twisted how I read scripture. I saw God through other people's broken lenses and my past experience, but now the blinders were off and I was beginning to experience Him for who He really is. Good. Loving. Abundantly generous. One of the biggest lies I believed growing up was that God was disappointed in my dreams. In my younger years, with my misguided understanding of who God was and my "role," now that I was a Christian, fear gripped every decision I made. I was afraid I would disappoint God with my dreams because they were too "secular" and not "spiritual" enough. So, I stopped dreaming. If there was something good in my life, I just "knew" that God was going to rip it out from under me because He didn't want anything in my life competing with Him. I was afraid to be happy and find joy, and there was definitely no point in opening my heart to love anything because God would take that away too. I didn't allow myself to pursue my dreams because I judged them as worldly. God wants us to be successful and happy, and yes, holy too. He wants us to live the blessed life because He wants to set us up for victory and He knows His ways are good. That doesn't mean bad things won't happen or that there won't be persecution. He is not the author of evil. The enemy comes to steal, kill, and destroy. He comes to give us the abundant life. He redeems all the enemy seeks to destroy. We have a Father who loves us and is for us and will never leave us nor forsake us. He promises to use everything that comes through our lives for our good. By walking with Him, we learn how to live prosperous lives – mind, body and soul. God is not a cosmic killjoy. He is the best friend you could ever have. He is not your earthly parent or a cruel dictator waiting for you to fail, so He can punish you as you squirm around trying to figure out His will. He is not there to rip the rug out from under you when you experience joy and happiness either. The Bible says in His presence there is fullness of joy (Psalm 16:11), but He wants to release those things that bring us lasting joy and remove things that lead to our destruction. Dying to self means remembering I am already dead and raised to new life in Christ. It means, resting in the fact that I don't have to play God. I can rest in Him.

No longer playing God meant I was free to allow God to be God and discover what His will really was. Instead of asking Him, I just assumed my dreams were worldly because they required so much money. I believed Matthew 19:24, that it was *"easier for a camel to go through the eye of a needle than for a rich man to enter into the Kingdom of God."* I definitely wanted heaven, so I reasoned that being rich on this earth was out of the question. However, this scripture is speaking about where a man puts his trust. If it is in his wealth, well then, that's the wrong source. Scripture is not saying you will not enter the Kingdom of God if you are rich. Life in the Kingdom is about living from the Source. My dreams involved building family businesses, travel, a massive property where people could come to receive healing, training, and the transformation they needed in order to discover their own dreams and destiny. I wanted to transform communities one family at a time. I have also always wanted a beautiful home with land my family could build on for generations. I was all about transformation and influence, but I didn't allow myself to think outside the church building when it came to spiritual things. Ministry was a word reserved for the church, but really, it is just a way of life. In whatever you do, minister. **When we equate ministry with what we do in church alone, we begin to believe He can only use our gifts and talents in a church building.** People who don't always fit in, either spend their lives feeling like a square peg in a round hole, or they leave the church because they can't find their place. Yes, serve on Sundays. Come to be equipped and to encourage those around you, but don't limit your ministry to the four walls of the church building. Let me tell you, Evangelists make excellent salesmen. Apostles make great CEO's. Use your pastoring or teaching heart to feed and encourage the homeless, counsel a newlywed couple, teach a course on parenting or finances. The list goes on. Sometimes we buy into the belief that only pastors and worship leaders can operate in their gifts at church and all others are relegated to the nursery or chained to children's ministry. Allow those who shine serving in those ministries to do so. Just be aware, the body of Christ needs to function outside the church walls as well. The face of church, as we have always known it, needs to change. If the way we were doing things was working, then cities would already be transformed. We need to do something radically different. The church building is an equipping center to send out the ministers into the marketplace where the people are. Wherever you go and whatever you do, minister. Bring the kingdom with you and transform the world.

Through this deception, I had silenced a big part of how I had been shaped to "minister". When we equate prosperity with worldliness, we have bought the lie that God wants us to be poor. This belief is completely self-centered and doesn't take into account that God wants us to prosper in life, not just for ourselves, but for the sake of others. We actually have a moral obligation to be blessed. How much help to the poor can we truly be if we are poor? Consider the words of 2 Corinthians 9:8. *"And God is able to make **all** grace **abound** to you, so that having **all** sufficiency in **all** things at **all** times, you may **abound** in **every** good work."* That is a lot of "all's" that He wants us to abound in. We have a good work to be about and He wants to give us an abundant supply to accomplish it. When I started to open up to the idea of dreaming again, I delved into Scriptures looking for every reference to money I could find. There have been some extreme teachings on prosperity. I wanted to find out what God had to say about it and not just what I had been taught. It wasn't that I was money hungry and finally had the freedom to go after it, I was actually giving God permission to connect me with the dreams He placed in my heart and dismantle any limiting beliefs preventing me from stepping up. I knew I had to renew my mind about money so that I could be free to say yes to God when it came to stepping into my destiny. I never want anything "religious" to get in the way of my destiny.

When we become judge of our own lives, we walk in error. We are not meant to be God and it is not up to us to decide how much money is too much money. Money is not to replace our trust in God, for it is not the source of our security. God is our source. The resource may change, but our Source never does. He alone has the right to lead us into what abundant prosperity looks like for us. He wants us to prosper. After all, prosperity is not what you have—it's Who you have. He does not prosper us so that we can walk around like a proud peacock, but to invest in His Kingdom and be about what is on His heart. We are a funnel from heaven to this world. We are not about building our kingdom, but His. Jim Baker, of Wealth with God, has an excellent definition of prosperity. "You have no financial debt, more than enough money to fulfill every divine assignment God has for you, and enough left over to help others fulfill their divine assignments." Imagine what a witness Christians would be to the world if this was our reality. Family, we need to look different than the world. We need our lives to make others thirsty because of our saltiness. 3 John 1:2 states, *"Beloved, I pray that you may prosper in all things and be in health, just as your soul prospers."* He has no limits to how much our soul can prosper. He calls out to His beloved to prosper in ALL things. He wants us to be in abundant health. He wants our souls to be abundantly healed. Do you believe this? Can you imagine God saying, "That's healed enough. I want you to remain a little bit sick and depressed, and oh yes, you definitely need to be poor, so that you don't get too big in your own head." That's just cruel and totally against His nature. He is the God of abundance and complete transformation. He is a perfect Daddy that wants to set His children up for victory. How that will look is dependent on the destinies He has for each child, but He wishes *"that you may prosper in all things and be in health, just as your soul prospers."* This implies that the more we prosper in our souls, (our mind, will, and emotions) the more we will prosper in life. I remember when Troy just got out of seminary and we started ministry. He felt so disillusioned by the fact that he thought he was going to be leading an army, but instead, was in charge of a hospital. We need to do the work church. There is a world out there desperate to know God and be known by Him. Does God have the answers to the world's questions and problems? Are we living those answers? Do you not think that there is a world hungry for these kinds of answers? Everyone wants to prosper and be in health. When we live prosperous lives, we model for a world that we know the Answer. God does not make us sick to teach us a lesson. He does not keep us broken to humble us. Poverty is not spiritual. **He wants to bless us so that we can be a blessing.**

"God is our source. The resource may change, but our Source never does."

Does God Choose Our Toothpaste?

In the movie *Interview with God*, which is centered around a conversation between two characters, God and Paul, God draws out the deep questions in Paul's life in order to set him free. Paul thinks he is interviewing God, but God uses the opportunity to delve into the deeper questions Paul is afraid to ask. God says to Paul, "Your life is not an audition for the afterlife and if you could stop worrying about that you just might have time for other things. Things like loving one another and living your life." That is not to say there aren't consequences for the choices we make here in this life. All our works will pass through fire, but if we focus on works, we won't truly live. We will be centered on ourselves instead of walking in relationship with God.

God's intent was for us to believe His words and trust and obey so that we can live the life He intends for us to live, like in the Garden of Eden. When Jesus came to earth, He came to reveal the heart of the Father. He says, "If you have seen Me, you have seen the Father (John 14:9). His entire point of coming to earth was to reveal the heart of the Father and reconcile His children back to Himself. Religion paints a completely different picture which leads to separation, but Jesus came to demonstrate the love of a perfect Father and lead us to Him. Jesus came to model the Spirit-filled life, die on a cross to exchange our sin nature with His perfect nature, and purchase the keys back from the enemy with His blood. He did this so that

He could hand the keys to us to reestablish our reign on this earth once and for all. Salvation was only the beginning. Salvation happened at our convergence with the cross. But do not forget. Jesus was resurrected. He didn't remain on the cross. He stepped into the resurrected life. This is what the Kingdom is all about. So many Christians remain at the cross when there is a resurrected life to be lived. He wanted to restore us to intimacy with the Father through a resurrected relationship, not a set of rules. He did it all. It is finished. It's all about Him. He gave His life and we give our lives in return. We are saved *from* an eternity in hell apart from Him, but we are saved *to* a new life, a new nature, and a new purpose and destiny. We are saved to a resurrected life of love, power and a sound mind. We are free from fear and striving and instead, we enter into rest (Hebrews 4:10-11). We were created to take dominion and tend and care for this world He gave us to explore. We are not orphans. We are invited into a family and are a part of a love story that is so amazing; it's a no-brainer to give my life to Jesus.

In the above movie, Paul was struggling with the sovereignty of God. He was angry that God was not doing anything about the problems in this world. He goes on to accuse God of not helping him when he prayed. He didn't know who He was and what Jesus had accomplished on the cross. He didn't know his inheritance. He didn't understand sovereignty. Paul wanted God to tell him what kind of toothpaste to use, so to speak, and God was telling him that he (Paul) was more powerful than he knew. God was encouraging Paul to stop expecting that fixing all of life's problems like famine, war, divorce, etc. were His (God's) responsibility alone. God told Paul to be the miracle. Plant more food. Stop the war. Heal the marriage. Make the phone call to reach out. We are more powerful than we know. We were created to take dominion. God lives in and through us. We are His hands and feet. We are His voice and His heart. We are His image bearers. He is our Father and when we spend time with Him, our hearts conform to His and our desires change. We live out our free will because we choose to live the blessed life. Not because we had to, but because our will becomes His. God is sovereign, but that doesn't give us permission to be passive.

So many Christians live a passive faith waiting around for God to choose their toothpaste. Due to a misconception of the Sovereignty of God, they shrug off their responsibility to be accountable for their personal beliefs. They become victims rather than active participants in this life and then blame God that life didn't turn out the way they planned. God wants to partner with you on this journey. He wants you to know Him and not base your life on your experiences, but rather adjust your life to make room for the Truth of His Word. If you are a Christian, He is in you and beside you. He is there to talk and counsel with. He is there to help you climb your mountains and take your hills. He wants you to walk in the abundant life and in the more that He spoke about in John 14:12. Jesus is perfect theology. He is the example of all that is possible. We shouldn't settle for anything less. He is in every creative thought and dream and wants to activate you for life. Consider those in the world that are not believers, and yet they chase after their dreams and make them happen. They pursue life because that is an intrinsic part of their created makeup. We were all made in the image of God. We all have the Star-Breather as our Creator. He is an artist, mathematician, engineer, writer, doctor, lawyer, artisan, carpenter, businessman, investor, life coach, homemaker, etc. You name it and He is it.

"So many Christians remain at the cross when there is a resurrected life to be lived."

Image Bearers with a Destiny

We are not all children of God, but we are all created in God's image. The difference between unbelievers and believers is that believers have been awakened in their spirits and have had new life breathed into their eternal beings. They become children of God and not just created in His likeness. Believers actually become image bearers transformed into the image of their Father. They possess an entirely different nature. God transforms His own. So much more takes place at the moment of salvation than we are aware or are even taught from most pulpits. When we are born again, God takes the marred semblance of an image and restores it to its original splendor. Believers are saved from an eternity apart from Him and saved to a life originally set forth in the garden...to take dominion and tend and care for this world. We were created to rule and reign. That is a powerful God-given position. Being a Christian is no namby-pamby way of life, and unfortunately, many Christians take a back seat and shelf their dreams out of fear because they have an improper picture of God and His heart for humanity. He didn't send Jesus to save us so we could become religious. He sent Jesus so He could exchange what sin had destroyed, take the keys back from the enemy and place them back into the hands of His children. He wanted to restore us to Himself so we could be about building His Kingdom on earth. Now I call that a family business worth selling out to.

He Looks Her in the Eyes

God is good and this fact is another foundational truth that we must embrace. Because God is good, we are too. We no longer recognize ourselves as a lowly worm, because He does not see us that way. A groom does not look down at His bride. He looks her in the eyes. We have a new created nature that comes with a new paradigm for living. We no longer have to die to ourselves; we reckon ourselves dead already and alive in Christ (Romans 6). We no longer have to work for anything; we rest in who we already are. We laid ourselves low and were humbled as we nailed our old natures to that cross with Christ. Our old nature and identity are dead. Therefore, our identity is no longer a sinner, but a saint. We need to learn how to carry ourselves like royalty; by renewing our minds to think and act like royalty. We will reflect what we believe, so start believing you are His bride and you will hold your head high.

God Wants a Family

God didn't want puppets. He wanted a family. He wanted relationship. In our own families we as parents are not commissioned to be dictators, but protectors. We train our children toward the path of blessing and success. We want to set them up for victory. We want them to choose the path of blessing that we put before them because they trust our hearts. We don't want them to be compliant and make the "right" choices out of fear of disappointing us or for fear of punishment if they don't. As children get older, they have less rules and more responsibilities, but also more freedoms. By the teenage years, children should be fully trained, by loving parents, to know right from wrong. They should have learned social skills, etiquette, and how to be good citizens and healthy individuals. We give them identity and lead them to the God that loves them. We eventually become their mentors and the friends that walk beside them. We are there when they need us, to live life with, but we do not continue to make the decisions for them. They do not get up in the morning still asking us what kind of toothpaste to use. If they did, we didn't do our job well. We are to train our children to be competent adults that make good moral choices and love God with all their heart, soul and mind. We train them to live interdependent lives with God and others, but not passive lives. We train them to discover who God made them to become and bloom. We do not teach them to conform. We celebrate their diversity and cheer them on to their destinies.

The choices that they make become their own. We cannot control them any more than we can take responsibility or credit for what they do. We train, release, and mentor. If they choose a path that we do not want for them, well now we know what it is like to be God, who has watched many of His children wander from the path of blessing He has prepared for them. I am sure it breaks His heart when His children find themselves in brokenness and disillusionment from choices that sometimes have significant consequences. Is that because God failed? No. Is He to blame? No. When we honor God by raising our children in the way they should go, (Proverbs 22:6) then we are no more disqualified as parents for the choices they make than God, who is perfect, when His children choose a path that He did not desire for them. We each are given free will to walk our own path. We are all responsible for our choices and our reactions to the choice's others make around us. We are powerful people. Free will gives us that power.

Walking My Free Will Out in the Spirit

It's all about living in relationship with Jesus, not keeping a set of rules. I know I run the risk of being repetitive…too late, but this is good news here. I want this to sink in. We don't have to perform. We don't have to live lives of penance and self-deprivation. We have the free will to believe God and take Him at His word and follow Him all the days of our lives. Get yourself out of the way. Living for Jesus is using my free will to believe I am a new creation, and choose the blessed life. I trust, with child-like faith, that His ways lead to victory and success. That's wisdom. For example, maybe there is a song that you just love, but its message causes your heart to wander and drift towards selfishness, fantasy, discontentment, or strife. We have the free will to listen. It doesn't change how God feels about us or our eternal destination. We are not cursed for participating. He is not waiting to punish us. He allows us to make our choices as well as deal with their natural consequences. So, in your choice to listen to certain music and open yourself up to the messages in those songs, God is not to blame when we lash out at our spouses and children because they are not worshipping us or when our life is not the fantasy the world portrays it to be in the movies or songs. We opened ourselves up to a worldly, "me-centered" perspective that does not bring blessings. We open ourselves up to those things that cloud our view of ourselves, God, and the people around us. We make choices every day and those choices have consequences, good and bad, and that is what living life is all about: the freedom of choice. What may be a temptation for me may not be a temptation for you. That is why we can't make laws out of gray areas. We need to walk by the Spirit. I know my weak areas and so does the enemy. I need to be self-governed in my choices and not inflict those same disciplines to those around me. We need to take responsibility for the choices we make and stop blaming. You are more powerful than you know. He can use even your mistakes to work together for good (Romans 8:28). That's a promise.

Living Under a New Covenant

This is such good news. We have a Father that loves us and will help us make good choices when we talk to Him about life and everything we are going through. We have a relationship. We don't need to make "religious" choices that box us all in. The Pharisees did that. They took God's ten laws and made 613 out of them. That is legalism. God knew we couldn't even keep the ten He gave us. They were not meant to be kept, but to be a mirror of what we had become so that we would receive Christ's free gift and exchange our sin nature for His perfect nature. We are living under a new covenant now. We get all the benefits that Jesus paid for. We don't have to worry about messing up because the New Covenant was not between God and us. **The New Covenant was made between God and Jesus on our behalf, and because we are in Christ, we receive all the benefits that are His.** Anytime you add law to this grace, you contaminate it and put yourself back into the Old Covenant of law, to which you have to perform perfectly in order to be blessed. You already are blessed. The New Covenant is about who you already are and what you already have, through Jesus. The gospel is simple. It is God's invitation to enter into a relationship with Him that He intended from the beginning.

We don't have to wonder what God wants. We can talk to Him. He speaks to us all the time. He speaks through His Word, people, nature, experiences, signs, and that still small voice. Sometimes He even speaks audibly, like He did to me when He told me Troy was coming and I knew He was bringing me my husband. We have the privilege, as loved children, to choose God's best. He doesn't make the choices for us, but He does want to play an active role in His children's lives. He leads us to so much more. He leads us to joy. He leads us to true prosperity. I had grown up believing that I had to choose one thing or another. I couldn't have both. I was raised, as were many, on an Old Covenant foundation. In the Old Covenant it was A+B=C. God did His part and we do ours. If we perform perfectly, then we are blessed, and if we do not, we are cursed. So many, including myself, wonder what the good news is when we still mix grace with Old Covenant law. Folks, that isn't good news. That is a toxic mocktail when one is expecting refreshment. On this healing journey, I have learned it's not salvation or free will. It's salvation and free will, and I no longer have to perform for His love or acceptance. I already have it. I live under a covenant of grace through Christ. It is the goodness of God that leads us to repentance (Romans 2:4). When we overcome the obstacle of a religious mindset, and heal the orphan and poverty spirit, we get to choose His will, with Him by our side, because it leads to the best life, no matter what obstacles life throws our way. We no longer have to perform, but rather, rest as loved children of the King of kings. There will be trials and temptations, but we don't go through them alone. We step into the most wonderful relationship with God and the most amazing adventure ever. We build His Kingdom on earth with Him. Our faith and free will are a beautiful gift. **God is not dead... Religion is.**

Secret #12

Free will was God's idea. Separate the man-made god of religion from the God of the Bible.

Secret #13

God is good.

Secret #14

Eat from the Tree of Life, not from the Tree of the Knowledge of Good and Evil.

CHAPTER SEVEN

Your Past Does Not Define You: Exposing the Obstacle of Living from Your Past

When we delve into the reasons for why we can't let something go, there are only two: an attachment to the past or a fear of the future.

~Marie Kondo, The Life Changing Magic of Tidying Up

The fourth obstacle that needs to be exposed is the obstacle of living from our past. I have a watercolor picture in my kitchen of a little girl looking up and holding her heavenly Papa's hand. He is strong, all dressed in white, and facing a calm ocean. The title of the picture is "So Much More". It reminds me to trust and know that He is my Daddy God, my Papa, and I am His special girl. I am flooded with peace when I look at it. It reminds me of a now-healed memory that used to govern my entire life. Throughout my life, I kept revisiting this memory trying to find some way to fix it and finally heal. From it I had believed I was a daughter, but not family. I had an orphan spirit. As a result, I lived my life from the crumbs dropped from the table, believing if I could just be good enough, I would somehow be chosen and loved and have the family I longed for.

155

That belief transferred to my relationship with God; giving me an improper view of the Godhead, which hindered my Christian walk. When I finally took Jesus to that memory I was in turmoil, but as I looked at Him, He stood secure, unshaken and unsurprised. I remember feeling that if He could be secure and unshaken, then I could too. I so wanted to be like my Daddy God. When my body relaxed, He turned to me and said, "I have so much more for you." It took me two years to realize I never asked Him what the "so much more" was. When I later asked Him, He turned with my hand in His hand and we walked in the opposite direction. He told me to not look back. Like Lot's wife, who transformed into a pillar of salt when she turned back and looked at her past, we cannot preserve the past. Salt is a preservative and the past is not to be preserved, it is to be built on. The "so much more" is not found in the past because the past does not define us. He explained that I needed to give Him that memory and He would replace it with all of Himself. I was trying to get something from a past that was no longer there. That chapter of my life had closed and I needed to move on. **As long as I was focused on a dead past, there would be no life in my present and no hope for a future.** By turning away, I was able to let it go and trust that God had an inheritance for me as His daughter and I hadn't missed out on it. He had a place for me at His table, and I was His loved daughter and part of His family. I haven't looked back and you know...He does have so much more for us...more than any earthly family could ever give.

Now let me be clear. I love my parents, they are amazing and I am very happy with my relationship with them, but even the best parents aren't perfect. I know I am not. Remember: your parents were also parented by imperfect parents. We all need healing from our past. We all need "parenting" in the present. As a side note, I want to add that there is no need to feel guilty for having identity issues if you feel you had the most amazing parents in the world. God wants to heal all our wounds no matter how big or small. Never feel guilty in thinking your issues are not as important to God by comparing your issues to someone you think has it worse than you.

God treasures each of our hearts where we are and He has enough room in His heart for all of us. We live in a fallen world. By default, we are going to get messages contrary to the truth while growing up. The point is, these messages need not define you. Only God can perfectly heal those broken areas of our souls. Any longing we have will be completely satisfied in Him. The cool part is when those needs are met in Him, anything this world has to offer becomes gravy and we can finally live from a place that is free to give and serve others. **When we have soul wounds, then we spend our time distracted by licking them and building upon a broken foundation. But when we are healed, we are free to enter into life.**

When I Was a Child...

We have such an intrinsic desire to know God and be known by Him, but oftentimes we get stuck in the past. We have either been labeled or have labeled ourselves. These labels form what we believe to be our identity. God wants to reveal to you who you really are. The past does not define you. I shiver to think of the person I would be right now, had I let my past define me. I was told some pretty harsh lies that I believed for much of my life. I focused on perfecting the only things I felt I had going for me, hoping to make up for the lies I believed. Because identity is key to breakthrough, it is imperative to get your identity from God and allow Him to heal those childhood wounds so you can find freedom and not remain stuck. I took Jesus to those places where each lie had been spoken over me and I asked Him where He was. He stepped in front of me and received every harsh word. They were no longer spoken over me; He had taken them on Himself. He is an amazing Big Brother. That is the power of the gospel. It is a beautiful exchange of our ashes for His beauty and time is of no importance. God is in our past, present, and our future and so is His ability to heal.

Children believe incomplete things when they have no one to process their pain with. They form judgments, see only a partial truth, and naturally self-protect. The Bible says in 1 Corinthians 13:11, "*When I was a child, I spoke as a child, I understood as a child, I thought as a child; but when I became a man, I put away childish things.*" Many times, things happen to us in our childhood and our souls remain stuck there. Our bodies grow, but our soul wounds remain at the age of wounding. It is only when pressed that these areas surface and materialize. We can push them down, but the Bible instructs us to do away with childish things. We need to deal with our pain and trauma and find truth. Inner healing is a process and many times it is best to do it with a wise counselor or friend. We need to learn to confront and process each hurt that is triggered in our lives, get to the root, speak to God about it, and get His perspective of truth on it.

Inner healing is a humbling process. We become vulnerable and open ourselves up to areas that are not our strengths, because those areas have not been allowed to mature and we will need to depend on the strength of others to walk us into wholeness. It is so important to have a safe, Spirit-filled community, or friend that will allow you to be open and real. Most inner healing runs deep and the issues that spring up are young soul wounds that will, in turn, be processed from that youthful perspective. I am talking probable ugly crying here. Children process without inhibition most of the time, and like I said earlier, those inner wounds were buried in a child's soul and just stuffed and pushed down for years. Many of us fear addressing them because we don't know what will come up and out. Fear of the unknown and being out of control will cause you to stuff it back down. But it will always be there, and continue to govern areas of your adult life from a child's perspective, as my childhood wounds governed me. Deep wounds keep our lives anchored in the past, even if we believe we are pushing them down and out of sight.

"Deep wounds keep our lives anchored in the past, even if we believe we are pushing them down and out of sight."

Letting Go and Forgiving

Another key to overcoming the obstacle of living from the past is deciding to let go of people we have loved and lost, or people who have brought us harm. Many times, the things people have done to us have been horrific and damaging, leaving in their wake broken pieces and shattered lives. When we forgive, we are not saying what they did to us was okay, but rather, we give up our right to play God and cast judgment over them. We give up our gavel, and He gives us peace in return. He is allowed to be the

Father who is good at taking care of His children. We no longer have to carry the pain and bitterness that suck the life out of us and rob the strength from our bones.

Forgiving doesn't mean reconciliation either. Forgiveness is between you and God. Reconciliation is between you and the other party. We don't need to reconcile, but we do need to forgive. Unforgiveness only hurts you. Rarely is the other person even aware of the offense. God tells us that He will forgive us as we forgive others (Matthew 6). There will always be people to forgive. It is better to remove the triggers that keep us in the cycle of unforgiveness. When we know how much we have been forgiven, how much we have been given through our inheritance, and how good and worthy He is, there is no offense worth holding on to. I have a little quote on my refrigerator by Jaime Cross, CEO & Founder of MIG & the Her Effect ®, that reads, "Taking daily action to let go of the things that don't serve your mind, body, or soul." It reminds me to let go of anything that hinders my walk with Him as we walk together toward the "so much more."

Regrets and "If Onlys"

Regrets are another drain on life. Regrets are only unforgiveness against the self. Anger turned inward becomes depression. I had regrets that kept my focus on trying to heal my past. I kept fantasizing about going back and fixing those decisions. I once had a dream that I went back to those places in my life and corrected all my regrets so that I could arrive in my adulthood whole. In my dream, I arrived at the place where I met my husband and we enjoyed our year together as friends. When it came time for him to propose, he never asked. I distinctly remember knowing that we had children in our future, so when he didn't ask, I asked him when he was going to propose. Shocked, he explained that he only wanted to be friends and nothing more. I had so changed, that when it came time to meet him, I was no longer the same person he was originally attracted to in real life. In my dream, I panicked because I realized that all my children and the life I loved would disappear. I awoke suddenly and heard God speak that I was never to regret and meditate on the "*if onlys*" in life again. His promise is that He weaves it all into the beautiful tapestry of our lives. Even our mistakes He forms into a work of art. I have learned there are some things I can't change and need to let go of, but many things that I believed were unredeemable, are actually still possible. God told me to stop fantasizing about how I would do things differently. He told me to do things differently now. It wasn't too late to learn to play the piano or dance. It wasn't too late to buy that jeep or take that trip to Europe. These dreams will come to fruition and I will appreciate them even more as an adult. I am taking an art class now and going back to school online. It is never too late to dream.

"Taking daily action to let go of the things that don't serve your mind, body, or soul."

Mental Agreements vs. Actual Beliefs

The best exercise I ever did to heal from my past was to take some time and go after my mental agreements, recording what I actually believed about God. I have been a Christian most of my life and over the years, I would say, I had a mental agreement with many truths of God. Those were truths in my head because they were the "right" things to believe and not necessarily what I actually believed. I wrote out three lists: what I believed about God, the Holy Spirit, Jesus, and on each list, how I thought they each saw me. I shared these lists with no one. This was an actual account of what really was in my head: my belief system. For instance, when I prayed, the first thing I would hear was, "I haven't heard from you in a while." That thought immediately condemned me, brought guilt, and put a wall up between God and me. With it came a slew of condemning thoughts about my performance and disappointment that I had somehow fallen short and failed at maintaining my "perfect image" and thus put Him out. He was busy after all and could count on me to not add to His list of things to deal with. I had an image of a small god in my mind. I tried to perform perfectly so I was not seen as a bother or in the way, but an asset…so failing was hard. I wrote this down on my list. I saw God as disappointed, wanting me to perform, condemning, etc. If that is what was surfacing in my thought life, then subconsciously that is what I believed. See how twisted and embedded belief can be and how easy it is to dismiss it and continue on the path of an unreconciled belief system? Because of it, I didn't want to pray. I didn't want to hear condemnation every time I came to Him. That was my prayer life for most of my Christian walk.

Now, I thought I believed God was a loving Father that I could run to and sit on His lap and tell Him all the things on my heart, but that was not the belief I actually practiced when I prayed, so I would hold myself back and guard my heart. I had a mental agreement that God was good, but in truth, I believed He was not good to me. What I really practiced in my beliefs was fixing myself first before coming to Him. I didn't want to add to His trouble and if I had problems, well… shame on me. After all, I had been a Christian for how long? I should be beyond this somehow. I would feel the need to work out my problem on my own, so that I could come to Him all fixed and He would be proud of me. Our subconscious beliefs are what we ignore because we have made mental agreements in our conscious mind and think we believe one thing, but live out another. **Our mental agreements are masks we wear to hide the truth of what we really believe.**

This exercise took me a year to process and was the catalyst for my discovery of the most amazing relationship with God imaginable. After compiling my lists, I was able to recognize how I had transferred my beliefs of my earthly family and childhood experiences to God. I then repented of believing lies about Him, forgave anyone that needed to be forgiven, repented of allowing my mind to be the devil's playground, and I asked Him to replace these lies with the truth. I asked God if we could, in a sense, start again. Repentance means to think differently about something and to turn the opposite way, but it also means to believe LIKE God about the situation and get His perspective. Believers don't just believe IN God; they believe LIKE God. For example, you will never hate what you trust. My friend Larry likes to use this analogy when teaching others about repentance. If we lie, it is because we trust it and believe it will protect us. We need to get curious about why we are trusting it. When we can truly see something for what it is, it breaks its power over us naturally instead of having to force change through sheer willpower. This is how we overcome addictions, break the power of lies, remove things from our lives that are harmful, and see obstacles for what they are…roadblocks preventing us from stepping into the deeper life.

"Believers don't just believe IN God; they believe LIKE God."

We are not going to get rid of what protects us unless we replace it with a greater protector. We need to see that God does not want us to lie because it places us on a path where we will always have to watch our back and check our story, and thus cause us insecurity and fear. It also sets us up for broken relationships, because no one can believe a liar. It promises protection and provision, but eventually leads to death and devastation. Until we see things from God's perspective and through His loving eyes, we will not be able to repent or change our thinking. The best we can do on our own is to feel sorry that we were caught. That is not repentance. That is self-protection at best. Believing like God means trusting that His ways are perfect and knowing that He wants to set us up for victory. When we repent, we exchange our faulty beliefs that lead to destruction, with His life-giving beliefs that lead to the abundance.

Getting to Know the Trinity

As I continued on my journey to know God and align my beliefs to His truth, I wanted to get to know Him for who He is from His own lips. I had questions about the Trinity. What role did each play in our lives? If they truly were three parts of one God and they each had their own personality, then I wanted to get to know each one personally. After all, I am a mother, a wife, friend, daughter, and now a Water Walker, and with each role I play a different part. I don't come to my children the same way I approach my husband and yet, I am still Rebecca. As I read the Bible, I marked down truths about Him in my journal as He spoke to me about everything I read. I literally would read a passage and have a conversation about it with Him. I do that with books and movies too, not just the Bible. In fact, now, I am in constant conversation about everything because I find His perspective to be perfect and it saves me much trouble. He wants to talk to us about everything on our hearts. He created us for relationship. He didn't create robots, but He made us to have fellowship with Him and He calls us friends. We were meant to walk in fellowship with Him, like we originally were in the garden. So that is what I do. I talk to Him more about everyday things and slowly open my heart to areas I have been self-sufficient in.

I literally was starting over in my relationship with God, because I wanted to renew my mind of all I had been taught and just let His Word form my belief system. I wanted to get rid of my mental agreements and work those truths from my head deep into my heart. I had a reasonable idea in my mind who Jesus is, because He has more human characteristics and was much more relatable than a "Gandolph" type Father God. Friendship and companionship had always come more naturally to me. My experience with my own father was one of friendship and companionship. Because I didn't live with him, I didn't know him as protector and provider, although I always knew he was proud that I was his daughter. Jesus was literally God in the flesh. He even stated that if you had seen Him, you had seen the Father (John 14:7-9). I would need to grow in seeing God as a Father who was my protector, provider, and giver of my identity. The hardest part of relationship with the Trinity is separating our previous ideas we gain from growing up with our own families or ideas we get from Hollywood, with the truth of who He is apart from our experience. No matter how good or bad that experience is, God is not human and we cannot transfer those attributes to Him. We are created in His image, not the other way around. In Isaiah 55:8-9 God says, *"For My thoughts are not your thoughts, nor are your ways My ways…For as the heavens are higher than the earth, so are my ways higher than your ways and my thoughts your thoughts."*

Through our journey, I was beginning to learn to come to God with practical issues and open my heart to depend on someone other than myself. I was learning who my Father is. Then it hit me, if God is my heavenly Father, then where do I go for mother questions? He is always good at leading me to the answers. I had been comfortable talking to God about theology or identity issues, but at that point in my life, He was a bit more intimidating when it came to personal issues. I think many of us grow up in church comfortable with Jesus, having mixed emotions about God the Father, but Holy Spirit seems too confusing to grasp. We may put Him on the shelf. He seals us at salvation and empowers us, but how do we have a relationship with the Holy Spirit and what role does He play? Holy Spirit's job is to teach, nurture and comfort. Sounds like a mother to me.

When it came to needing someone to mother the "mother", I just kind of pulled up my bootstraps and plowed through somehow. I had "girly" questions. They seemed silly, yet they were important to me. I wanted to know my style and what colors looked best on me. I wanted to learn how to rest more and nurture those neglected parts, and if it was even okay to want those things. I had questions about parenting, food, and health. I needed a mommy to "mommy" me. If people had father wounds, they could find their healing in Father God, but what about mother wounds or mother holes? It was through getting to know Holy Spirit that I began to understand how God is neither male nor female, but rather both. **God is the perfect family**. He is mom and dad and big brother. Holy Spirit became my constant companion, my mother, my counselor and my teacher. In my prayer times, while praying in the spirit, I would imagine sitting knee-to-knee on the couch with Holy Spirit having "girl" talks. As I prayed, I felt my mom holes fill up. I asked for interpretation of what we were talking about in the spirit and I would receive downloads to all my "girly" questions; things I never would have known, but brought such healing when I implemented them. You men can do this too. We all need a mother.

Since discovering this part of our relationship, I don't feel like I am doing the mother thing alone anymore. I have more energy to pursue personal passions like writing, photography, herbal certification, and traveling. I just have a peace and confidence in who I am as a woman. I now have a perfect family. My relationship with the trinity: Father God, Holy Spirit, and Jesus, all existing together as one God, is such a beautiful relationship of honor. The pressure is off everyone else now, and I can just enjoy people for who they are and not need them to be "fixed" so that my life can be easier. I don't "need" them, but I love them and I want them in my life. I am not draining those around me trying to get some need met that can only be fulfilled in Him. That is a free place to be.

We are all on our own journeys and when our lives are filled with the presence of God, we are free to love people where they are and help them walk to where they need to go. We can do this without becoming distracted by our own issues and unmet needs. Working through my past with God finally brought me peace, removed triggers, helped me let go of constantly trying to fix my past, and stopped the striving to have my needs met through people. I find my peace in God alone. He has become my best friend and the one I share life with. **When we let go of the past, then we finally let those little people inside grow up and come into maturity.** We can separate from our past and start the work of building our character,

Secret #15

The past does not define you...God does.

Secret #16

Clarify in your life what is a belief versus a mental agreement.

CHAPTER EIGHT

Come to the Table: Exposing the Obstacle of a Lack of Character

God will always take care of you, no matter where you are! That doesn't mean you are supposed to stay there. He has much better plans for you than the wilderness.

~Doug Addison

The fifth and final obstacle to overcome is a lack of character. Truthfully, this one obstacle encompasses many because character is composed of multiple aspects. However, I decided to group it together to address the fact that many people think they can advance in this life and still bypass good, godly character. The entire book of Proverbs is written to show you that you can't, so I only want to brush up on a few character issues in the hopes of painting a broad stroke of understanding for you. When you follow the leading of your heart to the "more," you will have to change, and in order to change, humility will be your greatest tutor. Proverbs 9:10 states, *"The fear of the Lord is the beginning of wisdom, and knowledge of the Holy One is understanding."* Remember when I defined earlier that the fear of God is about having the right perspective of who you are compared to Who He is? Well, humility is admitting you don't know it all, and wisdom is allowing the "Master Potter", and Lord of your life, to mold and shape your character into the one He envisioned before the foundations of the world. The vehicle for this transformation usually begins with a wilderness season, a season of pruning and stripping away of all that will hinder the final outcome. One of the main reasons I wrote this book is to be a voice in your life during the wilderness time, to help lead you through it, so you know you are not alone. I want to let you know, truthfully, what to expect, and I promise you there will be uprooting, sifting, and pain, but more importantly, renewal and great victory leading to abundant peace and joy. Your wilderness season will be determined by the factors preventing you from living out your destiny, as well as the call on your life. A greater call requires the ability to hold more weight. God does not want to give you anything that would crush you, so He gives you the time to increase your weight bearing capacity and build the muscles necessary to carry out your calling. Your wilderness time doesn't have to be long, but a loving father will make sure it is thorough. I implore you— just make up your mind to surrender and obey, because He really is good and He really does want the best for you.

"The fear of the Lord is the beginning of wisdom, and knowledge of the Holy One is understanding."

A Vessel to Hold Wisdom

We are powerful people with powerful choices. He is not unwilling to pour out blessings, but He must make sure your vessel is able to hold what He pours out. He wants to first form you into a new wineskin, knowing your old wineskin would burst under the pressure of the new wine He wants to pour in (Mark 2:22). Good character is not something that you can be zapped with. Like a fine wine or an artisan sourdough bread, it grows over time. Proverbs was written by the wisest man who ever lived, King Solomon. He encouraged his readers to, above all, acquire wisdom. Wisdom needs to do its work in you to prepare you to hold the abundant life that God wants to pour out. The world can offer you facts and knowledge, but only God endows man with wisdom. Proverbs 2:20-21 TPT encourages us to, ***"Follow those who follow wisdom and stay on the right path. For all my godly lovers will enjoy life to the fullest and inherit their destinies."*** Following wisdom leads to a fulfilling life and inheriting the destiny God has prepared for you to walk in.

Hearing His Voice

How are we going to know this destiny if we don't know what God is saying to us? It is so important to get alone with God until you think as one. I believe that is why He had us go on our adventure. At home, with all the distractions, it was hard to get time alone with Him. My friendships were my life, and possibly even an idol in my heart, and God wanted us to Himself. He wanted to quiet all the voices in my head until His was the only voice I heard. There was too much noise in my head and too many voices of reason. There is only one voice when you step outside the boat that bids you to come. All other counsel simply confirms what He says. But you have to know His voice first.

Hearing His voice takes practice, but is essential to our faith walk, especially if you want to walk on water. God does still speak to us, and not only through His written Word, but through our thoughts, pictures on our mind, or impressions on our heart. He also uses: circumstances, dreams, visions, angelic encounters, people, and nature. He is God and He can do whatever He wants. The point is to learn to hear and recognize His voice, in its many forms, because He wants to communicate with us.

Yosemite Tourist

This reminds me of when we were camping at Yosemite National Park. We were all wading in the water near the falls where the raft tours ended. The children enjoyed watching as boat after boat arrived and the tourists unloaded. All except one boat. This was the last stop before the rough waters and another waterfall. As the boat approached, the tour guide called them in. They just smiled and waved enthusiastically, and continued talking as they floated downstream. The tour guide yelled again, waving her hands for them to come in. They waved back. It became apparent they did not understand English, and just thought the funny lady was being extra friendly. They continued to float downstream heading for the falls. Now the tour guide was adamant and ran into the water, while throwing a rope toward their boat. It landed within a few feet of them. They all continued to speak louder and point to the rope, but nobody grabbed it. She threw the rope again and this time it went over the raft. There was still no response. It was obvious there was a huge gap in communication. They just smiled and continued on their joy ride, laughing at the funny lady throwing the rope. I am sure they thought our American hospitality quite odd. With the third throw, the tour guide was up to her waist in the water, and now all of us on shore were doing our best to wave them in. At long last, they did finally catch on right before entering the rough water, however, not knowing the language could have cost them dearly. What efforts could have been spared had they known how to communicate with the one who could direct them and keep them safe. God wants to communicate with us. Learning to listen and distinguish the voice of God from the enemy, and from the voice in our head, our flesh, is vital.

An Invitation to Intimacy

In our family we have what we call Bramblet127 times. In the mornings, we gather together to read and meditate on Scripture, sing, make our declarations, soak in His presence, practice our spiritual gifts, enjoy family read-alouds, and receive blessings. In the evenings after dinner, Troy will read to the children and we all share what is going on in our lives. We try and make time with each of the children to have "nuggle" nights, where we just snuggle or talk about what is going on in their lives. When there are discipline issues we come to the table and work through them until things are resolved and a plan of action is established. We are a family, and families gather at the table and live life together. Remember, God did not create puppets. He created families. So, we are to model after Him. We have a loving, heavenly Father who calls His children to come to the family table, as an invitation to intimacy. It is at the table that we have the best family discussions. It is at the table that you learn that you are a son or a daughter of the King.

I can pretty much meet with God anywhere. I love intimacy with the Father and I am regularly in His presence. Remember when I told you Troy and I were different? Well, here is a major difference: I am a connector. I love details and long, deep conversations. I love romance and anything cozy. Troy is the opposite. He is a "go get 'em" man. Just give him a task and he will get it done. He loves to check off lists and prefers the bullet points to any conversation. Now, that's not to say he isn't loving and gentle, and totally fun to be with. He is an amazing man and is fully present when you are in front of him, but it's "out of sight, out of mind" when you're not. I tend to carry people and their issues with me and shepherd their hearts. We work great together, but it has taken time to develop this dance between us. We had to learn to value and appreciate the personalities and gifts of the other, realizing that we each had what the other needed in order to bring balance to our natures. My butterfly tendencies were more grounded by my rock of a man and my flying offered him a better view from above. He is the vision caster and I fill in all the details. All that said, whenever we discussed intimacy with the Father, Troy would get these uncomfortable images of a bride kissing, reclining, and wasting time. Troy had a hard time picturing himself, as a man, snuggling up in the lap of God. Some guys can, and more power to them, but my guy ran from this idea of intimacy and vulnerability. That is until we came up with the table. He could get his mind around a table discussion. He could imagine sitting having intimate discussions with his heavenly Father — no kissing necessary. Just being real.

Prayer is Just a Conversation with God

When we have an issue that we need to talk about together with our Father, we come to the table. The table needs to be a safe space to come as you are and process life, enjoy fellowship, laugh, share, delight, and unwind. It is a place to seek wisdom as well as strategy, a place of nourishment as well as conversation. Prayer is just a conversation. We need to lose our religious idea of prayer, so that we can start delighting in conversations with God. When we see God clearly, for Who He is, we will enjoy having conversations with Him. Remember He is a perfect Father wanting to set His children up for victory. He gives abundantly more than any earthly Father could (see Luke 11:13). He loves being in the details of our lives. I love this quote by Martin Luther, because it clearly depicts how I see the Father when it comes to prayer. "Prayer is not overcoming God's reluctance, but laying hold of His willingness." Isn't that beautiful? He really is a willing participant in our conversations. When we see Him as such, someone fully engaged, delighted, attentively listening, and interested in contributing strategies and solutions to the issues in our lives, then coming to the table in prayer with our Father can be a wonderful family time. When Troy and I come to the table, we close our eyes and imagine we're sitting at a large wooden table. My mind, of course, creates a beautiful space to meet. I picture pretty curtains, pictures on the walls, with snow falling outside. In my mind's eye, I create a cozy space to engage. You get the idea. In steady, black and white fashion, Troy just comes to the table. He doesn't need the fluff, but the fluff is fun to me. Neither are right or wrong. I am demonstrating how different personalities can engage in prayer at the table. However you choose to come, just come. Since starting up our business, we have needed wisdom and strategy from our "Mentor". We just come before

Him and lay out all our questions. We picture God, not only as our Father, but as our investor, mentor, and business partner. We ask Him His thoughts and perspectives. We ask for strategies and wisdom, making sure our motives are pure so we can hear clearly. We pray in the Spirit and then write down what we see and hear. We ask our accountability partners for confirmation if it seems way out there, but in general, it is no different than our evenings or mornings gathered around the table living life together with our children. When you get a proper picture of God, it is easy to place Him in those roles, even if you did not have that growing up. Remember, God is not your earthly parents. He is not even the best version of the greatest human you can think of. *"For my thoughts are not your thoughts, neither are your ways my ways," declares the Lord. As the heavens are higher than the earth, so are my ways higher than your ways and my thoughts than your thought."* (Isaiah 55:8,9).

"Prayer is not overcoming God's reluctance, but laying hold of His willingness."

Character Training is Part of the Deal

Character is purged under fire, and I am so thankful for the purging in our lives because without it, our vision would end up crushing us. Our gifts will make room for us. According to Steve and Wendy Backlund, just because an apple tree is not bearing fruit does not mean it is not an apple tree. It means it is still in process, but is an apple tree all the same. Consider the analogy of an iceberg. It's the 90% below the surface that sinks the ship. If you think of your gifts, talents, and skill as the tip of the iceberg, the 10% above the surface is what is visible to all around. Then consider character being the 90% below the surface. Without character to ground you, your gift or mission, talent or skill will float around aimlessly and dangerously. When character is developed, it will be your anchor and grounding to properly support the visible 10%.

If pride, childishness, ingratitude, self-centeredness, or idolatry were left to rule and reign in your life, these traits (which are opposite of Kingdom qualities), would destroy anything you tried to build. Let me tell you, when you step out of the boat, it is an invitation to a sifting. I am just going to be upfront with you. It is not an easy life at first, but it is a deeper life. It is not comfortable, but it is intimate. It is not predictable, but it is an adventure. When you surrender to God on the journey, character training is a free course that comes with the package. There is no better character training than through prayer with your Papa. You will pray as you have never prayed before. You will contend for your promises and labor to enter into rest. You will die to the things that will get in the way of your destiny because hopefully, through prayer and confessions, your mind will become renewed. When you have to wait patiently for answered prayer you develop the character quality of patience. You also learn steadfastness and humility. But there is a reward for your patience. God is faithful. I love what Pastor Bill Johnson says about prayer in his book, *Raising Giant Killers* (p19): **"If your answer to prayer is delayed, it is gaining interest.** And when breakthrough comes, it will come with greater power and glory than if it had been released at the moment you first prayed." I would also add, you will have gained the character to maintain it. Amen and Hallelujah. We are counting on it.

Sowing and Reaping

It's time to take a quick detour for a little gardening analogy. Since we are learning about the importance of character, I think taking this issue to the garden is the best way to bring it home. I have a desire to become a master gardener not just in the natural, but in the spiritual as well. I am learning how to steward the seeds I plant, instead of just planting them and hoping for the best. We steward seeds with our faith, which is active. We don't just plant a seed and hope it produces a crop; we expect it to produce. We nurture that seed through care and expectancy, not neglect and denial. So many believers have not learned how to one, sow seeds, and two, care for the seeds they have sown. God took me into the garden and showed me how easy it is to plant cucumbers. It doesn't take much faith or risk to plant cucumbers. Generally, they are a "set it and forget it" crop. Anyone can grow and produce a harvest, but who needs a thousand cucumbers right? Sure, there are plenty to share, but it's not what I really want to grow. It is just what is easy to grow. I get overwhelmed with the idea of learning how to plant and care for things like garlic and broccoli, apples or boysenberries. It takes an investment of time and energy to really study, plan, and prepare for how to get the best harvest by caring for those seeds and plants, as well as the proper time to plant in the first place. It is not as simple as planting a seed. It takes intentionality. It also means caring for that plant if disease strikes or pruning is required. Denial just pretends nothing is happening and only focuses on the expected crop. Faith, partnered with wisdom, seeks to find the solution and steward the crop so that you get the most from your harvest, not only to feed yourself, but also have an abundance left over to share with others.

I want to intentionally master each plant that I want to produce. This takes the character qualities of patience and diligence, as well as great wisdom.

I have avoided learning how to grow certain plants, not because I don't like them, but because they seem hard and complicated to grow. That is just a lack of skill and wisdom. I want to study and become wise and then work at putting my wisdom into practice. James 2:17 points out that *"Faith by itself, if it does not have works, is dead."* Of course, this applies to the spiritual and financial realm as well. Troy and I didn't understand the concept of sowing and reaping when we started out on our journey. We were always givers and generous with our time, talents, and finances, but found there is more to stewardship and sowing and reaping than just giving away a seed. It needs to be planted and nourished in good soil, watered with our intercession, and surrendered to the Son. On this journey, God showed me why my harvest is not always consistent, even though each spring I am excited about planting, preparing the soil, and yes, even weeding. I shy away from complicated issues like soil ph, beneficial plant pairings, thinning, fertilizing, etc. Attempting to master all the plants at once is overwhelming, but mastering one plant at a time is a step in the right direction and I will eventually see my garden flourish.

We can also look at character as being a seed we plant in the garden of our heart. Growing good character takes time and diligence. It doesn't happen haphazardly or overnight. The wonderful thing about character though, is that once your character is transformed it becomes a part of you. You are a garden in which your character grows. What you don't transform, you will transfer to those around you. Your character, in a sense, becomes the perennials in your garden…the fruit you see year after year. I am enjoying the perennials I planted and cared for years ago that are producing on their own now, with abundant fruit. I am maintaining my harvest, and my work has paid off in the form of a near passive harvest each year. When we submit our garden to the Master Gardener, we can begin to weed out those plants that are not desirable. Maybe there are plants that others have seeded into you. Maybe they are seeds you have planted yourself through your words or poor choices. It doesn't matter. You are in charge of your own garden and the harvest you desire to produce.

"What you don't transform, you will transfer…"

Sowing and reaping takes time to learn, not only in the natural, but in the spiritual as well. Galatians 6:7 warns, *"Do not be deceived, God is not mocked; for **whatever** a man sows, that he will also reap."* What you sow into the Kingdom you will reap. I love the word "whatever" here. When you sow seeds of time, you reap time. Just look at the harvest produced from investing time, or not, in your children. Do you have close relationships or are you distant and fractured? Look at the seeds you are sowing. When you sow financial seeds, you reap financial blessings. What is the state of your finances? Does it reflect the seeds you have sown, maintained through good stewardship? If not, maybe you have not learned how to sow financial seeds. We were always givers, but didn't know how to turn our money into seeds. When you sow seeds of joy, love, kindness, faith, and compassion, you reap an abundant crop of those things. Farmers plant seeds expecting a harvest of the seeds they plant. We can't expect a harvest from something we have not planted, nor should we expect to harvest apples when we have planted cucumbers. If you sow seeds of doubt, fear, selfishness, greed, negativity, and hate, then you have a picture of the garden you will produce. It is important to get an actual account of what you are sowing. Take a good look at your character, your words, your beliefs, as well as your harvest and evaluate in honesty, with the leading of the Holy Spirit, what seeds you are actually sowing and into what soil you are sowing them. Why do you think all of life started in a garden? Our words and actions are seeds. These seeds need to be nurtured, fertilized, watered, and given good soil with lots of sunshine to thrive. What kind of gardener are you and what seeds are you planting into the soil around you?

Praying Perfect Prayers

God has some wonderful tools for training. When we come to the table, we come as His children. It says in Proverbs 13:24 that a father who loves his son will correct him. Father God trains and equips His children. Not only does He give us the five-fold ministry for the equipping of the saints (Ephesians 5), but He also gives us spiritual gifts to use to grow us up into maturity. Read 1 Corinthians chapters 12-14 to learn more. Every believer is given at least one spiritual gift. Every believer is also given a prayer language when they are filled with the Holy Spirit. I didn't always believe this. I didn't find value in a prayer language and was ignorant of its power, but it is definitely a secret to overcoming any obstacle.

Before we had started our journey back in 2009, I had met a young woman named Rana. She was about my age and newly saved. God had put His finger on her and wanted me to reach out and offer to disciple her. She was artistic, from a Catholic background, and knew nothing of religious protocol. She was fun to disciple because she had the faith of a child and read the Bible ravenously. She had the right idea. She looked at God's Word as her inheritance and invitation into all that was hers. It wasn't a list of dos and don'ts to her. She had grown up in religion, so this invitation to a relationship with God was new and exciting. We met every Monday evening for "couch time." One evening she came with questions about tongues. She got it into her head that all people should speak in tongues. I did not possess this gift at the time. Nor did I want to, because I had no paradigm for the gift except that I knew it caused trouble and that it sounded weird. Not my cup of tea.

In her quiet time, she told God that if it was a gift He wanted all to have, then by all means, give it to her. She came to me excited that God had given her the gift of tongues. In my interpretation at the time, I thought speaking in tongues was when someone stood up in church and said something in a funny language and then someone else was supposed to stand up and interpret it. She kept arguing that we all can speak in tongues. We went round and round until I finally realized, through studying the Word and not what I had been taught, that there is a difference between the gift of tongues used in a public setting, and a prayer language. When a believer is filled with the Holy Spirit, the Holy Spirit comes in power and gives us a language to communicate with Him. When we pray in the Spirit, we are personally edified and our faith is built up, as it refers to in the Bible in Jude 1:20. I am not trying to get into a theology battle here. I am only speaking from my experience and what I have studied, not from reading books and others' interpretations, but simply by asking the Holy Spirit to open my eyes to the truth. When I finally understood the difference, Rana laid hands on me and prayed that I would receive my prayer language, not the gift of tongues. That night changed my life. My spiritual daughter laid hands on me to impart a gift. How awesome is that when our "children" run with what they have learned from us, make it their own, and then turn around to pull us up higher?

I received my prayer language right around the time we were asked to leave our previous position, and with all the emotional upheaval going on, I didn't know how to pray. One night I had such fear of leaving. With all the emotions of how we were leaving, there was such a burden on my shoulders I could not carry. I was pregnant and hormonal. I was trying to be faithful, but sometimes didn't know how to give the situation to God. So, I prayed in the Spirit. I prayed and wept from deep within. I didn't know what I was praying, but I was getting it all out and placing it in His hands. After I prayed for about a half hour, I felt emptied of the burden. He then told me to go to sleep. I slept better than I had ever slept. I was learning how to live out of control because He was in control. Romans 8:26-27 paints a beautiful picture of praying in the Spirit, *"Likewise, the Spirit also helps in our weaknesses. For we do not know what we should pray for as we ought, but the Spirit Himself makes intercession for us with groanings which cannot be uttered. Now He who searches the hearts knows what the mind of the Spirit is, because He makes intercession for the saints according to the will of God."* We can pray perfect prayers because the Holy Spirit is praying the perfect will of the Father through us. Now, I was free to pray perfect prayers and my mind didn't need to perform by saying what I thought was the right thing to say. I had a baby knowledge of my prayer language. As time would pass, I would learn that praying in the Spirit would be one of the biggest secrets to the walk of faith, as well as the joy and power in the adventure.

Fasting the Flesh

When you combine prayer with fasting, you are decreasing the flesh and increasing your spirit. For over fifteen years, I could never do a water only fast, because I was always either pregnant or nursing. When I finally did get the chance to do a water fast for three days, I loved it. I loved whipping my body into submission. I loved the strength I felt inside telling my body to submit. The flesh craves and we just obey it like we are feeding a wild beast. I never realized how many times I put chocolate in my mouth throughout the day. It is the best feeling to have self-control instead of being controlled by the flesh. Just a side note, by fasting we are not trying to kill the flesh. It is already dead, remember, we are new creations in Christ. Fasting brings the body into proper alignment with the truth. Fasting is a time to starve the flesh and remind it that it has been rendered powerless and dead at the cross. We walk in the resurrection. Because we live in a world that feeds the flesh, it is good to take time to remind ourselves how in our weakness, He is strong.

Troy's Fasting "Retreat"

Back in 2011, Troy decided to go on a spiritual retreat in the mountains for a ten-day water fast. He had done several three-day fasts, but felt God calling him to meet Him in the mountains. When he arrived home, I wasn't prepared for what shuffled through the door. He was a shell of a man, all hollowed-out and frail. His skin hung on his face. Now, I don't say that to throw you off the idea. Troy's experience was not normal. Each experience is different. He has fasted since and it hasn't been as dramatic, but this time God was doing some major heart surgery. God had done an amazing work while he was in the mountains. Troy conveyed to me that he had no strength and was only able to lay on the couch. He took a few walks, but mostly he just laid there and prayed. At one point, he remembers lying on the couch and watching Jesus perform surgery on his abdomen. He said Jesus kept pulling things out of him with a giddy smile and throwing it over his shoulder. He thought he must have been hallucinating due to a lack of food, but when he came home, he was literally liquid love.

Crushed by the Weight of Glory

We were in the presence of pure love and yet, none of us knew what to do with it. It was uncomfortable and time consuming. It was vulnerable and intimidating. It brought such a conviction that I knew nothing of love. I had no reference for my experience. It reminded me of the time God woke me up to pray for the neighborhood I lived in. His heart and presence came down on me and I thought I was going to die. I couldn't get low enough to the floor. His love for my neighbors consumed me till there was not a thought of myself. I begged him to release me because I could barely breathe. I had wanted His heart for the lost, but when I got a tiny bit of what I asked for, I could not hold it because His heart is so great, so vast. We have no idea what we are asking for. If He gave us all we asked for, it would crush us, unless we were able to push through the process required to hold the vision He wants to release. This was similar. Troy had been in the presence of God and He was changed. The problem was we had no paradigm of what to do with the transformation, so he ended up reverting back to his usual ways. Love is vulnerable and exposed. I had been used to living with a guarded man and the taste of love I had experienced was too much for me to endure. It crushed me. I was too self-centered, enjoying my own comforts and freedoms, to carry the gift that was given to me. It has been many years since that time. We have spent much time soaking in the presence of Love so that it is not so unfamiliar now. We have made Him the center of our world and now our world centers around Him.

Foodie Run Rampant

We live in the world, but we are not of it. You don't have to look far to see how the world has been swallowed up in lack of character issues such as gluttony or entitlement. The "foodie" culture, with its food addictions and pleasure-guided gastronomy, runs rampant, leaving people living without self-control in what seems like a worldwide, acceptable norm. I am guilty of loving food too much and feeding the tongue more than my body. I am not saying food is bad or evil. God gave us a bounty of choices for our health, good pleasure, and nourishment, but living out of control lives and giving in to every whim is harmful on many levels. There is a balance. There are amazing books written on the subject of food and health; one of my favorites was written by my friend, Dr. Scott Stoll. His book *Alive* not only addresses food and how it is so connected to our physical health, but he addresses it on a spiritual level that is powerful, easily digested (yes, another pun), and convicting. We read his book as a family and have been making shifts in our eating habits. We are enjoying the fruit of not living under the power and control of food, but we are still in process. I will always be a "foodie" at heart because food is such a part of life, connectedness, and culture, but it doesn't control me like it used to. There is a fine balance between health and celebration. I had been leaning toward the celebration too much and my body was paying a price. I don't want anything in my life that controls me or that I put before God, because it will ultimately hurt me. I want my life to be under the control of the Holy Spirit alone.

What Do You Believe About Money?

Just like enjoying food is not wrong, but rather a matter of self-control, what we believe about money, prosperity, and wealth is a matter of character as well. Ridding our hearts of the lens of poverty is a matter of the life and death of a dream in the Kingdom. Greed, lack, false humility, selfishness, presumption, entitlement, poverty, ingratitude, idolatry, and poor stewardship are all heart issues that will lose their ground when your mind is renewed with a proper understanding of the Father's heart. I have addressed the topic sporadically throughout my book because it is important. What you believe about money is foundational for establishing a Kingdom mindset and walking on water. It is imperative to address it under the obstacle of character because Jesus spoke often about money and for good reason. The love of money, otherwise known as mammon, will destroy us, but the proper view of wealth and prosperity will allow it to be a tool that will lead others into a relationship with an extravagant Father who loves to bless His children. What you believe about money is a reflection of what you believe about God. Jim Baker, in his book titled *How Heaven Invades Your Finances: Book 1: Build the Foundation for Supernatural Finances,* makes the argument that money is an intimacy issue,

> *The whole purpose of money is to draw you into greater intimacy with God. If you have wealth, you will need the revelation and strategy of what God wants you to do with that wealth. If you are building wealth, you will need the revelation and strategy of what God wants you to do with what you have. All of life flows out of intimacy with God." (p 4)*

"...money is an intimacy issue."

When God gives you a Kingdom vision, it requires financing. Remember what I said earlier about our God being a wealthy investor looking for managers to steward His wealth? God wants to finance the Kingdom through godly stewards because when righteous people have money, they do righteous things with it. When we have the right character and belief about money and we walk in a spirit of excellence, we attract the attention of heaven as well as the world. Proverbs 22:29 points out, **"Do you see a man who excels in his work? He will stand before kings and not just mere men."** I also love Proverbs 11:10-11: *"When it goes well with the righteous, the city rejoices: and when the wicked perish, there is jubilation. By the blessing of the upright the city is exalted, but it is overthrown by the mouth of the wicked."*

Money is not evil, but an improper view of it can be devastating to the Kingdom. God wants to strongly support the righteous. He wants them to prosper and have a proper view of money. Afterall, there is a world watching and the "church" has the answers. A large majority of the church operates in a poverty spirit (viewing life through a lens of poverty) and it is simply not biblical and does not reflect the nature of God. This confusion surrounding money is an issue of contention that I believe we should press into. I will address issues of contention later in chapter 10. There are bad examples in the church of misuse and selfish affection toward money, but truthfully there are bad examples outside the church as well. This is not an excuse to bury your head to the truth. We need to know what the Word of God speaks about money for ourselves and align our lives up with the truth rather than depend on regurgitated beliefs of one standing behind a pulpit on Sunday morning alone. We are held accountable because we have the Word and we need to steward His truth and challenge our beliefs if they do not line up with what we have been taught. Remember, our experience should not define our theology, but rather, our theology should define our experience. If we have character issues regarding money, it will be an obstacle in reaching your destination as well as an obstacle to a watching world.

The Glorious Exchange

We need to realize that what we believe affects the entire body of Christ and ultimately a watching and hungry world. Our actions flow from our beliefs. We need to stop competing and start watching out for each other's souls. We need to speak life over each other and call one another up. If pride, jealousy, greed, selfishness, or any such vice exists in us then we will not be as effective. This does not mean the answer is to read our Bibles and pray more. It means we read our Bibles and pray differently. We are not praying and fasting to get victory. We already have it. We pray in agreement with heaven until it manifests. Capps' quote is worth repeating, "I tell my people they can have what they say, but they are saying what they have." Don't come into agreement with what you have, declare the promises of God and move in the opposite spirit.

Remember that the cross was all about exchange. We get to exchange what we encounter on earth for what is available to us in heaven. Don't allow your feelings to lead you. Lead your feelings. When your flesh feels ungrateful, go on a gratitude walk and remind yourself of all the things you have to be grateful for. If you are acting childish, grow up, and put behind you your childish ways. If you battle with self-centeredness, go out and serve. Bring the homeless food or blankets. Put yourself in situations where you can see that life is bigger than just your perspective. If pride rears its ugly head, then immediately take the humble posture. Do the exact opposite. If you are in an argument and offense pops up and strokes your ego, realize that relationships are more important than winning. Listen instead of defending. Don't interrupt. Treat the person in front of you as the most valuable person in the world. They are to God. Realize you are serving the King of kings when you serve the person in front of you. Treat them as you would Jesus Himself. I guarantee you will speak differently. We need to hold ourselves accountable for our beliefs as well as our actions. Be responsible for governing your own character and take personal responsibility for your own life. Don't make excuses anymore. Excuses are only lies we tell ourselves that keep us in bondage.

"This does not mean the answer is to read our Bibles and pray more. It means we read our Bibles and pray differently."

Do Hard Things

Character and integrity matter. Move in the opposite spirit of your flesh and don't be afraid to do hard things. This is work, friends. There was only one disciple who stepped out of the boat and Jesus did warn in Matthew 7:14; *"Narrow is the gate and difficult is the way which leads to life, and there are few who find it."* That doesn't necessarily mean they will not inherit eternal life, but they may arrive on the other side of time, not fulfilling what they were created to walk in. I don't want that for myself, nor do I want that for you. I encourage you to fast from things you feel entitled to until your soul comes into alignment with the truth. If there are idols in your heart like food or movies, money or music—fast from it or give it away. Intentionally remove the idols from your heart so that you are not controlled by anything.

Idols of our heart can get in the way of us stepping into our destiny. For example, I knew I loved movies too much. They were my escape and the way that I brought peace to my life apart from God. I felt entitled after a long day of homeschooling my children, cooking, and cleaning to "veg out" and escape in front of the TV. There is no such thing. I decided to test myself, get curious, and actually stay engaged while watching a program one evening. This time, I paid attention to what was going on in my body: how I was feeling, what thoughts were racing through my head? Was I really relaxing? Was I really giving myself a treat? I noticed all the agendas, ungodly images, attitudes and subliminal messages my subconscious was taking in while "vegging." I noticed that I felt stressed, irritated, and dumbed down. This wasn't a treat. Nor was it "vegging out." My subconscious was fully engaged and my thoughts and emotions were responding even though I chose to tune out. I thought to myself, "What a waste of time." At least for that particular show, I was feeding my mind things that were directly contrary to what I was desiring to grow in. So, I let it go. Nowadays, I just watch movies on occasion. I decided I liked "vegging," but I wanted to think like Jesus more. Through just being curious and tuning in, I was able to stop a behavior naturally instead of feeling like I was depriving myself of a treat. I didn't want it anymore after discovering it wasn't serving the purpose I had originally thought it was. In addition, I wrote a list of exciting possibilities…things I could accomplish, now that I had all this free time on my hands. Writing this book was one of them. I wrote and published a book instead of "vegging." How about that?

Walking on water is going through the training of the wilderness time so you can reign in the Promised Land. The best way to do this is to come to the table and talk with your Father God. Find others of a like mind to come to the table with you and be your family. The Christian walk all comes down to belief. What you believe is powerful. Your actions display your beliefs. When you are believing for "the more" and you step out of the boat, your first steps will likely land you in a wilderness. Don't despair, even Jesus was led into the wilderness, right after He was baptized and just before He walked in the fullness of His destiny. A key to His success was that He knew His identity. At His baptism (found in Matthew 3:17), His Father declared over Him, *"This is my beloved Son, in whom I am well pleased."* Knowing His identity was His secret to keeping His eyes focused on the Father He knew loved Him and was worthy of His trust.

Path to the True Riches

Jesus came to lead us on the path to the true riches of God. I love what I heard Bill Johnson say once; "Earthly riches will buy a person a meal, greater riches multiply one meal to feed five thousand." Earthly riches are a step to reach the true riches. If we are not faithful to handle the little things, we will not be able to steward the greater. Our finances are the little things. What we do with our money reveals where our heart is. When God knows He can trust our hearts to be generous and wise with what He has given us to invest, then He will entrust to us the true riches. I believe the true riches are intimacy and communion with the Father. This is that sweet spot when your heart and the Father's are one. Intimacy with the Father becomes the greatest treasure. It is from intimacy that we move in the supernatural. I encourage you to study the parable of the talents found in Matthew 25:14-30 in light of this. We can have earthly riches, things we can do in our own strength. We can feed the hungry, raise money for widows and orphans, and pay a hospital bill. Those are all generous things and they all require sacrifice. Or we can follow Jesus out onto the waters and multiply one meal and feed five thousand, eliminate poverty in a whole city, or clear out a hospital. That requires supernatural faith. That's where we want to go, but it starts with faithfully investing what is already in our hands first. The place for testing and establishing our beliefs is in the wilderness times. We can't circumvent this step. The wilderness reveals what you actually believe. There is no avoiding it and you cannot enter the Promised Land without it or the weight of your destiny will crush you.

"Earthly riches will buy a person a meal, greater riches multiply one meal to feed five thousand."

That is why God gives us mentors so we can learn from, prophetic words to encourage us in the direction we need to go, and even angelic hosts to minister alongside us. If it feels like you are in a wandering time and you have been forgotten, or your life is the complete opposite of the words you have been given, or if the dream placed in your heart, seems unattainable, know this is a time of testing and sifting, but also of preparing and equipping. Holy Spirit leads you into all truth. Not just by telling you truth, but by walking you through it experientially (John 16:13). This means that many times you will be put in the exact opposite circumstance of the truth. God wants to reveal Himself to you in a way than He couldn't before. He wants to have a fresh encounter with you. Every trial we face is an opportunity for an upgrade in our relationship with God and in our faith. Use this time to develop skills and increase in wisdom. Learn to ask the right questions. If you are not getting answers then maybe you need to ask better questions. "Why me?" is not a good question.

Don't just wait around for your prophetic words to "happen." Contend for them. In the words of my friend William Wood of Global Awakening, "Preach to the walls." He was called to be a preacher, but had no pulpit. He would someday, but in the meantime, **he preached to the walls and came into alignment with the picture of his future self.** The wilderness time is the most loving act of a heavenly Father possible. It is a gift. Look around at Hollywood to see what happens when money, fame, prestige, and recognition are given before there is a firm foundation to hold it: brokenness abounds. The Bible says in Proverbs 28:25 that *"He who is of a proud heart stirs up strife, but he who trusts in the Lord will be prospered."* In other words, if you have a greedy, self-centered heart, it will be to your own destruction. But those whose heart believes like God will prosper. God wants His people to prosper and the way to prosper is to be led through the wilderness to remove any obstacles (including character issues), that come between you and an intimate relationship with your heavenly Father. How long you remain there is entirely up to you.

God has so much more for us, but it requires taking a good look at our lives and deciding what we want more. Destinies don't come to couch potatoes unless that is the destiny you desire. Insanity has been labeled as doing the same thing over and over again expecting a different result. If you want something more, then you have to do something more. Stepping out of the boat into the more requires doing a total heart check. We need to evaluate the areas in our lives that we have not surrendered and ask ourselves why. Whose kingdom are we building? The Kingdom has a King and He has a right to the throne of our hearts because He knows how best to care for His own. Allowing our flesh to rule and reign in our lives will only lead to our destruction. **Don't settle for mediocrity when you can rule and reign in the Kingdom.** Come to the table and let your heavenly Father lead you into the abundant life free from controlling character issues that render you out-of-control. Come as you are but don't stay there. Grow up and walk with Wisdom.

Secret #17

Learn to hear God's voice. Get alone and quiet with God until all the other voices have faded, and it is only His voice you hear.

Secret #18

Fast the flesh. Soak. Pray in the Spirit. Worship. Journal. Declare. Repeat.

Secret #19

We fight from victory, not for it.

Secret #20

Grow up and walk with Wisdom.

Secret #21

Money is an intimacy issue. What you believe about wealth, money, and prosperity is essential to walking in a Kingdom mindset.

CHAPTER NINE

The Radiant Bride

I saw the Holy City, the New Jerusalem, descending out of the heavenly realm from the presence of God, like a pleasing bride that had been prepared for her husband, adorned for her wedding.

~Revelation 21:2 (TPT)

God longs to see such a radical transformation in His church. If we just believed we are who He says we are, how different we would look. He longs to remove the obstacles standing in your life that hinder you from becoming all He died and rose for you to become. He wants to replace fear with His perfect love, unbelief with faith and identity, a religious mindset with a living, vibrant relationship. He wants to heal your past so you can step into your present, facing a hope-filled future. He wants to radically transform your character so you look like Jesus. He is preparing you not just for eternity, but He is preparing His bride for His Kingdom and His Kingdom is at hand. His Kingdom is here. He purchased not only our lives at the cross, but the keys to the Kingdom. Those keys He brought back and handed to His bride. Let's take a closer look at His bride in Proverbs 31:10-31 (TPT):

THE RADIANT BRIDE

WHO COULD EVER FIND A WIFE LIKE THIS ONE—

SHE IS A WOMAN OF STRENGTH AND MIGHTY VALOR!

SHE'S FULL OF WEALTH AND WISDOM.

THE PRICE PAID FOR HER WAS GREATER THAN MANY JEWELS.

HER HUSBAND HAS ENTRUSTED HIS HEART TO HER,

FOR SHE BRINGS HIM THE RICH SPOILS OF VICTORY.

ALL THROUGHOUT HER LIFE SHE BRINGS HIM WHAT IS GOOD AND NOT EVIL.

SHE SEARCHES OUT CONTINUALLY TO POSSESS

THAT WHICH IS PURE AND RIGHTEOUS.

SHE DELIGHTS IN THE WORK OF HER HANDS.

SHE GIVES OUT REVELATION-TRUTH TO FEED OTHERS.

SHE IS LIKE A TRADING SHIP BRINGING DIVINE SUPPLIES

FROM THE MERCHANT.

EVEN IN THE NIGHT SEASON SHE ARISES AND SETS FOOD ON THE TABLE

FOR HUNGRY ONES IN HER HOUSE AND FOR OTHERS.

SHE SETS HER HEART UPON A NATION AND TAKES IT AS HER OWN,

CARRYING IT WITHIN HER.

SHE LABORS THERE TO PLANT THE LIVING VINES.

SHE WRAPS HERSELF IN STRENGTH, MIGHT, AND POWER IN ALL HER WORKS.

SHE TASTES AND EXPERIENCES A BETTER SUBSTANCE,

AND HER SHINING LIGHT WILL NOT BE EXTINGUISHED,

NO MATTER HOW DARK THE NIGHT.

SHE STRETCHES OUT HER HANDS TO HELP THE NEEDY

AND SHE LAYS HOLD OF THE WHEELS OF GOVERNMENT.

SHE IS KNOWN BY HER EXTRAVAGANT GENEROSITY TO THE POOR,

FOR SHE ALWAYS REACHES OUT HER HANDS TO THOSE IN NEED.

SHE IS NOT AFRAID OF TRIBULATION,

FOR ALL HER HOUSEHOLD IS COVERED IN THE DUAL GARMENTS

OF RIGHTEOUSNESS AND GRACE.

HER CLOTHING IS BEAUTIFULLY KNIT TOGETHER—

A PURPLE GOWN OF EXQUISITE LINEN.

HER HUSBAND IS FAMOUS AND ADMIRED BY ALL,

SITTING AS THE VENERABLE JUDGE OF HIS PEOPLE.

EVEN HER WORKS OF RIGHTEOUSNESS

SHE DOES FOR THE BENEFIT OF HER ENEMIES.

BOLD POWER AND GLORIOUS MAJESTY ARE WRAPPED AROUND HER

AS SHE LAUGHS WITH JOY OVER THE LATTER DAYS.

HER TEACHINGS ARE FILLED WITH WISDOM AND KINDNESS

AS LOVING INSTRUCTION POURS FROM HER LIPS.

SHE WATCHES OVER THE WAYS OF HER HOUSEHOLD

AND MEETS EVERY NEED THEY HAVE.

HER SONS AND DAUGHTERS ARISE IN ONE ACCORD TO EXTOL HER VIRTUES,

AND HER HUSBAND ARISES TO SPEAK OF HER IN GLOWING TERMS.

"THERE ARE MANY VALIANT AND NOBLE ONES,

BUT YOU HAVE ASCENDED ABOVE THEM ALL!"

CHARM CAN BE MISLEADING,

AND BEAUTY IS VAIN AND SO QUICKLY FADES,

BUT THIS VIRTUOUS WOMAN LIVES IN THE WONDER, AWE,

AND FEAR OF THE LORD.

SHE WILL BE PRAISED THROUGHOUT ETERNITY.

SO GO AHEAD AND GIVE HER THE CREDIT THAT IS DUE,

FOR SHE HAS BECOME A RADIANT WOMAN,

AND ALL HER LOVING WORKS OF RIGHTEOUSNESS DESERVE TO BE ADMIRED

AT THE GATEWAYS OF EVERY CITY!

The Proverbs 31 woman is not just a woman, but "The" woman, the Bride of Christ. I believe this passage gives a detailed picture of the end times bride that Jesus is preparing. Read through it again, through Jesus's eyes as He details His beautiful bride and co-heir. Whenever I go on my walks to pray and make my declarations, I pray from this posture, as His bride. This is also how I see people, because I believe it is how He sees us. When someone comes in to receive ministry, I am already catching a vision for how He sees them and how He wants to heal their perspectives. He is giving them new eyes so they can view themselves through the lens of the new man, not a crucified corpse in need of fixing. Galatians 2:20 states; *"I have been crucified with Christ; it is no longer I who live, but Christ lives in me; and the life which I now live in the flesh I live by faith in the Son of God, who loved me and gave Himself for me."* The old man is dead. Renew the mind and cleanse the soul of lies and you will walk as His radiant bride. Read how powerful and productive "she" is. This is the character I want, and the character I truly am, because I possess a new nature: the nature of Christ. This is who I am and so are you. So, manifest your reality and start living as His bride. Believe you are who He says you are.

A Matter of Perspective

I believe many read Proverbs 31 and think it is just for women, like it's a long, weighty checklist for a godly wife. And it is, sort of…but it is not just for women. We look at the passage and think it is something we have to do instead of be. In the natural, there is no way one woman can accomplish all of this unless she has many servants. Over the years, women have read this passage and felt burdened, like they have to become superwoman in order to achieve it. We can't do it in our own strength and we aren't meant to do it alone. Learn to look at Scripture not as something one has to do, but rather a book of your inheritance and all that you possess. Don't say, "I have to work till the wee hours of the morning to clothe my family in fine clothes." Rather declare, "My family is clothed in fine linens and my lamp never goes out. You are always working even when I sleep. You speak to me in my dreams and prepare me for the next day's adventure." Do you see the difference? One is a task. The other comes from a place of rest within a loving relationship. The Bible reveals our inheritance. Treat it as such and you will treasure every word. The Proverbs 31 woman is not just a woman, she is His bride. We are collectively the bride of Christ...both men and women. We are not in competition; we are one. We are all His bride that He is preparing.

> ## *"Learn to look at Scripture not as something one has to do, but rather a book of your inheritance and all that you possess."*

Mirror, Mirror on the Wall, How Does He See Us, One and All?

Let me describe how I believe God sees His Bride. When He bids us to come out of the boat onto the water, He is calling us to step into how He sees us and what He died to restore us to. This end times bride is our true identity. Can you imagine how the world would react to seeing the church finally stand up and become the bride? We see now through the glass shards of a broken mirror, but He has restored the mirror and calls you to gaze in and see what He sees, so you can rise to your true calling and destiny. He looks at you and sees the completed work of Christ in your new nature and all your glory. This is what He sees, so this is who you are. He is married to a victorious, restored, and born-again bride, but many still live in the shadow of the fall, viewing themselves through a broken mirror. Many still see themselves at the foot of the cross, in all their brokenness. Jesus died on the cross, but He rose again and so did you. Our old nature is buried in the tomb, but don't forget we have been resurrected to new life with a new nature. When we take communion, we are remembering what He declared in John 19:30 that "*It is finished.*" He took on every sin and curse, including poverty, sickness, disease, and limitation. Isaiah 53:4-6 states,

> *Surely He has borne our grief and carried our sorrows; yet we esteemed Him stricken, smitten by God, and afflicted. But He was wounded for our transgressions, He was bruised for our iniquities; the chastisement for our peace was upon Him, and by His stripes we are healed. All we like sheep have gone astray; we have turned, every one, to his own way; and the Lord has laid on Him the iniquity of us all.*

He took it all.

Your Kingdom Come...

Matthew 18:18 continues to empower us with the truth that "*whatever you bind on earth will be bound in heaven, and whatever you loose on earth will be loosed in heaven.*" If He took everything on Himself on the cross and died, and we died with Him, and if He was buried and resurrected to new life, then we are too. That is what I love about Isaiah 61, our mission verse. It is all about the glorious exchange. He did away with our old sin nature and anything that identifies with it. We walk in beauty instead of ashes, joy instead of mourning, praise instead of despair. As His bride we are ambassadors of heaven. Our mission is to exchange what we see on earth for what is the will of heaven (Matthew 6:10), *"Your Kingdom come. Your will be done on earth as it is in heaven."* We have the privilege of exchanging on earth what is contrary to heaven, bringing heaven to earth. There is no sickness or disease in heaven so we send it away and call forth health. Does it always work? Not yet, but I would rather believe and have one healed, than doubt, and have none at all. We walk in faith and step out as we see the Father moving. Jesus was moved with compassion and poured out His life, modeling a life that is not only possible, but His heart's desire. He is calling you out of the boat to become His bride. See yourself the way He sees you. Proverbs 31 is His victorious bride. She is you.

She Reflects the Nature of Her Groom

Let this sink in. I will paraphrase and expound on Proverbs 31, as well as incorporate all that I have gathered from Scripture, through a poem, on how Jesus describes His bride. She reflects His own nature. Remember how Jesus makes the point that when we have seen Him, we have seen the Father? Well, I believe, when the world sees us, they should be seeing Jesus. Ask yourself if this is who you are? The answer is yes, and the more you see yourself this way, the more it is realized in your life. This is why it is so important to confess truth over your life. Romans 10:17 states that *"Faith comes by hearing, and hearing by the word of God."* Let His words and truth wash over you and cleanse you of all that you have collected over your lifetime. In order to renew your mindset, so that you start believing like a bride, you must see yourself as the bride. Before you go striving to try and become her, realize you already are. She just needs to manifest. When something contrary manifests instead, that is when we make the exchange. This is who God sees when He looks at us, because we are covered in our Bridegroom's righteousness. **We just need to develop eyes to see what He sees, so we can become who we already are.**

She has strength and mighty valor. She knows her identity: mighty, wealthy, excellent, morally righteous, full of substance, integrity, abilities, and strength. She is mighty like an army; overcoming and victorious and full of wealth and wisdom. She is worth the price He paid to restore her life. She has purpose and destiny, an ambassador, and the hands and feet of Jesus on this earth. She destroys the enemy and takes back the spoils to further the kingdom. She is an exact representation of Christ, the Bridegroom. His heart is fully entrusted to her and she brings the rich spoils of victory and wise investments to lay at His feet. He will have no lack because his bride shares his heart and dreams. She brings Him good and not evil all the days of her life. Every decision is filtered through eternity. She searches out to possess what is pure and righteous. She guards her heart for everything she does flows from it – out of her mouth her heart speaks.

She protects the gateways to her mind (eyes and ears), and continually renews her mind with truth. She gives no place for lies that would lead her astray and rob her of her blessings. She delights to work with her hands. She is never idle, but rather looks for opportunities to serve and use the gifts she has been given. She feeds others with revelation truth and teaches all she learns. She is a reservoir of revelation truth. She lives and feeds herself from the secret place — a continual source of food for others. She is grafted into the vine. Circumstances don't define her or rock her character. She sees earth from heaven's perspective. She tastes and experiences a different substance and her light does not go out, no matter how dark the night. She buys wisely, is generous, lives with a spirit of excellence, and finds good deals on good things. She has no trace of a poverty mentality, but one of royalty and thinks as a bride, His bride. She is hospitable. She feeds her family with good, healing food. She prepares their temple (mind, body, and spirit). She is not lazy, but prepares for her days and uses her time wisely. She lives intentionally, not just for the moment or to satisfy the immediate gratification of the flesh. She does not let her emotions lead based on feelings, but rather leads her emotions to express gratitude and thanksgiving. She sows her seed in good soil and with the profits, continues to plant and set aside seed money. She does not plant her bread or eat her seed. She is wise in matters of wealth: investing her money, time, and talents.

She is a servant of the master, a daughter about her father's business, a bride building the dreams of her and her Bridegroom; she is one with Him. Living from peace, she knows He will work all things for her good and His glory. She speaks life over herself and those around her. Grace, like honey, drips from her lips. She knows how to bring beauty from ashes. She girds herself in strength, might, and power in all her works. She is physically, mentally, and spiritually fit, for her body is a temple for His service. She strengthens and cares for herself, a cup overflowing for others to drink from. She meditates day and night on His word. Revelation flows from her dreams. Her lamp never goes out. She is in constant communion. She lives a life of gratitude and thanksgiving knowing every good gift comes from above.

Problems are only invitations into the "so much more", for she wears heaven's solutions as her crown. Her environment, situation, and circumstances do not affect her strength and inner peace. She has a heart for the poor and needy. Involved in the affairs of her world, she speaks truth from a biblical worldview. She is known for her extravagant giving and she herself is always clothed in the finest: clothes that reflect her royalty, character, and position. Psalm 91 affords no fear of tribulation. At rest, she and her household are safely sheltered under His wings. She is covered in righteousness and grace, forgiveness and repentance. Her life preaches the gospel to those all around her, making Jesus famous in the land. She is not judgmental, for God is the only Righteous Judge. She eats from the Tree of Life, her continual source. In childlike innocence, she rests in Him.

She loves her enemies and has her Father's heart for them. With His eternal perspective, she laughs at the enemy, filled with hope for these latter days. Her teachings are filled with loving kindness, wisdom, and instruction. She is a watchman over her family, an intercessor for the world. She sets her children up for victory, raising them up to be prosperous, even as their souls prosper. She is raising adults, prepared to be sent out as world-changing, water-walkers. She is highly favored and enjoys the fruits of her labor. Not focused on what the world focuses on, she lives for an audience of One. There is good and then there is better. She is decisive and intentional and lives in the fear of the Lord, not in her vanities, chasing after things that will burn up. Her heart and soul are eternally focused. She will be praised throughout eternity for her wise investments. She has treasure in heaven and will eat of the fruit of her hands and her own works will praise her.

Now this is how I believe the church looks through the Bridegroom's eyes. The world needs the church to see herself the way He sees her. Wake up church, and be the gloriously radiant bride He says you are. Step out of the boat and leave it behind you. Walk towards your Bridegroom.

Secret #22

See yourself as God sees you, His radiant Bride.

Secret #23

Treat the Scripture as your inheritance

and treasure every word.

CHAPTER TEN

Don't Follow the Sheep in Front of You

———————— ⚜ ————————

What would you do if you were 10x bolder?

That is what fear and unbelief are keeping you from.

~Pastor Nataly Galichansky

I t was a beautiful, sunny morning on Mother's Day. We were in Oregon at the time, and my dad decided to take us to one of their favorite breakfast spots along the Rogue River for Mother's Day brunch. It was a perfect spot along the river. The pine tree air wafted in the cool breeze and the sun shone as the river carved its way along the bottom of the steep canyon walls with its gorgeous tall pines stretching to the heavens. I love Oregon. It is mostly blue and green. Sky and trees, and all the fresh air one needs to fill the lungs. It was a perfect day. We all gathered out on the back deck getting ourselves organized. The waitress brought out plates, silverware, and napkins and took our drink orders then invited us in to fill our plates at the buffet inside. I grabbed my plate and headed in, stomach leading the way. When I opened the door, in front of me was a large buffet table laden with steaming hot pancakes, sausages, bacon and eggs, fresh fruit, yogurt and granola. It was piled high and ready for the taking. The only problem was the giant line on the other side of the room leading to a buffet table that ran along the side of the kitchen. The line ran out the front door. I had come in the side door because we were sitting out on the back patio. Why was the line so long for the other buffet and yet this buffet was loaded with the same foods, and yet no partakers? I sat there for a moment, sizing up the situation and then decided to step out of the boat and lead the way around to this other buffet table. What happened next was amazing. All the people in the other line began to talk amongst themselves as if saying, "Look, that food over there is the same food in this line. Why are we waiting in this other line when there is food to be had over there?" Like herded livestock, led by a sheepdog, the line broke off and people slowly made their way behind me. They began dishing out their food with big smiles as they confessed being afraid to come to this line because nobody was here. They were used to following and nobody was leading the way. By stepping out and thinking for myself, I had invited them to a feast in half the time, and they were no longer following the cattle in front of them. They left the herd, and enjoyed a terrific Mother's Day brunch.

Leaders Lead the Way

I have always been a leader. I ask "why" a lot. Sure, it gets me in trouble and I am used to going against the flow, but it certainly has broadened my horizons and led me to some pretty amazing discoveries, as well as some deep relationships. In the above story, the benefit to asking why was that I didn't have to wait so long for my food. It meant more time with family and more time enjoying the beautiful view. Stepping outside the boat, when most would prefer to sit comfortably in it, is a narrow path that few tread. Those that walk this path are leaders, and leaders tend to gravitate to other leaders. They have big dreams and no ceilings. I know a big God who owns the cattle on a thousand hills. Yes, there are some leaders out there serving themselves and building their own empires, but not us. We are kings in God's Kingdom, partnering and serving the King of all kings.

Troy and I lead from a place of rest. We rest in our big God and the fruit is evident to those who know us. I am not saying we are perfect by any means. Those who know us well can vouch for that too, but we are always growing, always hungry, always learning. Mostly we just love God and love living the blessed life. He knows what He is talking about so we choose to listen…it's as simple as that! We don't choose to follow the sheep in front of us. We choose to lead the herd to Jesus, as any good shepherd would.

Once Upon a Time…

I hope that through the following recounting of a familiar story, I can contrast the world's humanistic worldview, as well as the religious mentality of much of the church, with the journey we have been on. My hope is to inspire you to move past the obstacles that stand in the way of your created destiny, empower you with the secrets to sustain it, lead you to further resources that will equip you on your journey, and offer encouragement as you build a godly heritage in leaving a legacy for the next generation to follow.

There once was a small and meek orphan, named Dorothy, who felt invisible her whole life. She longed to see life in technicolor and knew deep inside there was a world beyond the rainbow. She was aware that there was an enemy after her, threatening the idols of her heart. In a dream that night, her house was picked up by an enormous tornado and placed in a colorful land filled with little people. Upon arrival, after successfully killing an evil witch of the land, she was given a pair of ruby slippers to wear on her journey homeward. Although she had arrived in the technicolor world of her dreams, all she wanted to do now was go home. Freedom and adventure were too unfamiliar, and she longed for the comforts of home. She begins the journey homeward in search of the city of the "Great and Powerful Wizard of Oz" by following a man-made golden path, which begins in the land of the small people. Along her journey, she encounters three friends: a scarecrow who didn't know how to think, a tin man without a heart, and a lion without courage...all three looking to this world to answer their question, "who am I?"

Dorothy is ignorant of the power she holds in her ruby slippers, because nobody has discipled her regarding their use nor explained why the enemy would make such an effort to attain them. She was told she had to find out on her own through works. She was willing to give up those ruby slippers for the idol in her life (her little dog), unaware that the enemy was crafty, knew her weakness, and knew where to turn up the heat in order to get what she wanted. The four pals continued on their journey down the golden road towards the destination, Oz. The enemy, who held nothing back to prevent their arrival, cursed a field of beautiful distractions with a sleeping potion, causing Dorothy and one of her companions to fall into a deep slumber. She is awakened only by the help of the good witch. Upon arrival to the great city, they are denied access, until the doorkeeper realizes she is wearing the ruby slippers. Dorothy finally begins to understand the power of her inheritance, but it is only through continuing on the journey that she gains more understanding.

The four were immediately cleaned up in order to make themselves presentable to stand before a false god, who pretends to have power, but is impotent to perform. He requires works in exchange for his help, because in reality, he is scared of the enemy himself. They embark on a terrifying journey to the heart of the enemy, where they are ambushed by flying monkeys, who lock up the little orphan. She finally releases her idol and he runs for help. Meanwhile, time is running out and the enemy wants her inheritance. At this point, Dorothy realizes that the slippers are more powerful than she thought, and she begins to see their value. She eventually escapes, with the help of her orphan friends, and accidentally discovers the weakness of the enemy, which is water. The witch is dowsed in a bucket of water and melts. The kingdom is freed because the goodness of the little girl destroyed the wickedness of the enemy. She was wearing the ruby slippers.

As ordered, they bring the evidence back to the "Great and Powerful Wizard of Oz", only to find out he was a fake and phony all along. He was not a powerful wizard and he did not keep his promises. He tries to make up for his lack by offering his worldly wisdom to the hungry travelers, and sends them down the path of performance orientation because that is all his world has to offer. The scarecrow, who believed his identity rested in his intelligence, is told that a diploma from a renowned university will make him a great thinker. But in reality, it is only the attaining of wisdom and truth, and renewing the mind with right beliefs, that make one a truly great thinker. The tin man is told that "a heart is not judged by how much you love, but by how much you are loved by others." This will only lead him down a path of self-protection because he will learn that performance is the way to gain the approval of others in order to fill his empty heart, longing for love. True love is found in giving your heart away to another, Jesus, and receiving His heart in return. The lion, who began his journey singing, "If I were king of the forest…" was not acting courageously because he didn't know his identity deep within. Courage was already in his DNA, he just didn't know how to manifest it. He was a king living like a kitty cat. The world tells him that in order to be courageous, he needs to be a hero. Oz is right in that the lion is a victim of disorganized thinking, and gaining wisdom and changing his beliefs will make him courageous, but a medal is not necessary to be recognized as a hero. Dorothy gains friends and an understanding that she had the power to get back home all along, through her ruby slippers, but forgets that the journey has changed her. Unfortunately, she has not learned to dream bigger, but rather to remain comfortable. She lets fear govern her dreams and steps back in the boat because she has not learned the secrets to sustain her destiny. She has conquered many enemies, but still seems lost. Dorothy, the small and meek, as she likes to call herself, fails to know who she is and therefore remains small in her own mind. She might as well have stayed in the land of the little people. What Dorothy does not realize is that she has only viewed life from the shore and from inside the boat. She lives a life of either/or and doesn't stop to expand her possibilities and question life outside the boat.

It takes courageously stepping out into something, to see we do, indeed, have courage. It takes stepping out and thinking differently, to see there is another perspective. By renewing our minds, we can reprogram our brains to think smarter and actually bring heaven to earth. It takes stepping out to realize, that our hearts are much bigger and deeper than we believe and we are capable of changing the world. It takes stepping out of the boat to realize that there is a world of technicolor out there to be discovered. The destination, "home", is not a place, but rather a Person; Jesus Christ. And the answers for our deepest life questions can only be answered in Him.

Limiting beliefs often keep our world small. The movie *The Wizard of Oz* paints such a graphic picture of religion's answers for the Christian walk: striving, performance, works, living as an orphan, false responsibility, and the masks we wear so that we don't have to be vulnerable and exposed. We hide behind a curtain and project, with smoke and mirrors, fancy lights and flashing colors, an image that is unreal and will fail when tested. Do we not at times project ourselves as the "Great and Powerful Oz" when in truth, we feel like the man behind the curtain? We don't need to project ourselves as something we are not. We need to remove the mask and become who He already said we are. Religion is such a powerful demonstration of a journey leading right back to where you started, only arriving more disillusioned. Overcoming the obstacles of fear, unbelief, a religious mindset, the past, and a lack of character are imperative for the journey. We need to think and dream bigger. We need to remove the religious masks so we can see with Kingdom eyes. That is what we had to do and are still doing. Our journey was all about leaving Egypt so that we could enter our Promised Land.

A Key is in the Contentions

Like Dorothy, who didn't understand the power of her inheritance or why the enemy was after her ruby slippers, many never stop to look at the areas in their lives that are heavily guarded. The enemy is after the treasures of the Kingdom. He knows what is precious, and his goal is to keep us ignorant and slumbering, disunified and exclusive, secure in our ticket to eternity but making very little impact for the Kingdom this side of heaven. It's not the invaluable things that get the most attention. A key is in the contentions. If the enemy is after unity, then unity is probably important. If there is constant strife over the gift of tongues, healing, prosperity and finances, the end times, the relevancy of certain books of the Bible, such as the Song of Solomon or Revelation, then they are worth exploring. They must be heavily guarded by the enemy for a reason. Don't take man's opinions or interpretations as an excuse for not studying the Word of God on your own. We cannot allow fear of error to keep us ignorant of the truth. Truthfully, if you are turning a blind eye to areas of Scripture out of fear, you are already walking in error.

"...if you are turning a blind eye to areas of Scripture out of fear, you are already walking in error."

A Wake-Up Call from My Slumber

It was actually a challenge from a friend that opened me up to the deeper things of God. I was content to just hear a sermon on Sunday and think I was doing my religious part. What I heard on Sunday or at Bible study I just assumed was my opinion too. I didn't think for myself. I was just following the sheep in front of me. My friend had encouraged me to study a few passages of Scripture (1 Corinthians 12-14), which she believed proved that certain gifts were not used by the church anymore. Unfortunately, at this point in my life I couldn't have cared less because I didn't see that it affected me, since I was not using those particular gifts and had never seen them demonstrated by anyone around me either. So, it felt irrelevant. I was ignorant and self-centered.

My friend was adamant, so I took up her challenge and read the passages of Scripture she referenced. I studied them over and over, asking God what He thought. I still couldn't see what she was saying, since I was just reading the Scriptures naturally. In fact, it started a holy fire inside of me as I realized there was so much more to this walk than I had been taught or knew about. I became ravenous in reading the Scriptures and told God that I wanted all that He had for me. The funny thing was, when I approached my friend to thank her for opening my eyes to the truth that there was so much more, she responded that I was not supposed to come away with that. She then proceeded to hand me a book and said, "Here, read this book and you will see the truth."

I remember her gesture made such an impression on me because I realized she was taught to believe what she believed, just as I had passively been taught to believe what I believed. If I had to read a book about Scripture to be convinced of a truth, then it was just man's wisdom. We need to come to the Word with an open heart. Books are secondary and should always point you back to the Word. I know she believed what she had read in her book was confirmed in the Word, but so many times we let our experiences justify our beliefs, instead of challenging our experiences by aligning our beliefs with the Word of God. That's how it all began with us. We realized our lives were not lining up with what we read in the Word. He wanted more for us. He wants more for you. Books can expound on truth, but my advice is never receive truth blindly. Never let a book become your only theology. Holy Spirit is perfectly capable of leading us into all truth. I challenge you to take it to God and work through it. We cannot passively receive the teachings of man anymore, but instead test what we learn against the Word of God. Ask yourself, "Who told me that?" Deliberately go after truth and initiate the step out of the boat and dare to dream with God.

Learning How to Dream Bigger

I have always been a dreamer. In fact, I had a bucket list when I got married with very specific things I had wanted to do my whole life. These included things like tasting lobster in Maine by the sea, and ride a train into Boston, wearing a brown dress, and a hat while carrying a little bag. I wanted to ski and have blueberry pancakes with pure Vermont maple syrup in Vermont. I wanted to see the ice skaters at Rockefeller Center in NYC at Christmas time. These were all the East Coast dreams this California girl couldn't wait to experience. I dreamed specifically and my husband made sure all of my dreams came true.

My biggest dream was having a happy family. I wanted to see what a Christian family looked like with lots of children and a mom and dad that loved each other. With all my dreams fulfilled, I didn't know what to do but ask God for more dreams. Bigger dreams that require risk and are out of the ordinary. To me, the idea of growing up with a happy family was large enough. My ceiling was low when I was younger, and I thought I would be asking for a lot with this dream, as if God had limitations. We are the ones who have the limitations. Our heavenly Father is extravagant and longs to pour out blessings onto His children. He told me on this journey, after I had experienced so many specific dreams that I had desired all my life, that I would have what I longed for. It was up to me to renew my mind to think bigger, to increase my ceiling.

So many of us have limiting beliefs that cap our lives and keep us small and unable to dream. Maybe life for you became a matter of necessity and survival, but history is replete with examples of people who have defied their stations and financial limitations, as well as their physical handicaps and pursued their dreams. They did not let others' limiting beliefs hold them back. They were not victims of their past. They did not listen to the voice of mediocrity. It takes guts to step out of the boat and silence the voices. But look at the journey that awaits. You never know what you are capable of, until you try.

I asked my grandma one day, if she could plan her dream birthday, what she would do. Her answer shook me, because it revealed a limiting belief in my family line that now I was finally able to recognize and understand. She answered, "I would really love to go to Red Lobster."

Shocked, I came back with, "Grandma, you can dream anything. Why not lobster in Maine?"

She replied, "Oh that is just silly talk of dreams."

"Well then, let me be a silly woman," I thought to myself, "for I dearly love to dream." Dreams take pressing in. They don't come passively or accidentally. The next year we flew my grandma out to spend Christmas with us in New Jersey. We took her to see all the lights, the Rockefeller Christmas tree, and all the storefront windows of New York City. It was a dream she had buried that I just happened to catch wind of. She later told me she never thought it was possible to fly across country at her age (she is in her 90s), but she did. In doing so, she was able to dream of even more possibilities. Our ceiling rises with each dream fulfilled. So... Dream Bigger!

Troy and I already have big dreams and are continuing to learn to dream even bigger. We heard it all across country as we were stretching ourselves to define the vision God had for us. He kept telling us to dream bigger. How do you dream bigger when you are surrounded by the same things? I love the quote by Charlie "Tremendous" Jones; "Five years from today, you will be the same person that you are today, except for the books you read and the people you meet." We became voracious readers and enjoyed meeting people from all walks of life all across the country. There is a whole world out there and so many different viewpoints, but you will never see it if you only live in your little circle, or even your Christian bubble. That is why in my sheik dream, which I recounted earlier, I was offered the choice between staying with a dress already prepared for me, or stepping out on an adventure to make my own gown.

My gown now has wisdom, keys, anointing, memories, authority, diversity, spiritual gifts, encounters, new mindsets, other people's stories, and deep connections and lifelong friendships with people from all across the country. It's been an amazing adventure, and although it had some perilous moments and things I don't wish to relive, it has changed me. It has changed us and prepared us for what is to come. The wilderness times are the training ground for trust, preparing us to hold and sustain the destiny that He has planned. Embrace the process. In your wilderness season, use your time wisely and intentionally. Learn the lessons He has prepared for you so you won't have to repeat them. Clarify your vision. Seek wise counselors and mentors. Gain what you need to sustain the reign.

"Five years from today, you will be the same person that you are today, except for the books you read and the people you meet."

The Biblical Account of Joseph

In the biblical narrative of Joseph's life, found in Genesis chapters 37-50, Joseph is an amazing example of a man who learned to dream bigger. I want to contrast Joseph's journey with Dorothy's. We are on a Joseph journey. Many are....it just helps if you know it. Joseph had been given dreams of God's plan for his life. In his overconfidence and lack of experience, he interpreted them within the confines of his small world. He was his father's favorite, and for this reason, his ten older brothers conspired against him and had him sold into slavery, all the while telling their father he had been mauled by a wild animal. God was with Joseph. He was sold to Potiphar, one of Pharaoh's officers, and gained great favor as his integrity, character, and skill were recognized. Potiphar's wife seduced him, but because of his integrity and love for God, he rejected her, which resulted in his imprisonment due to false accusations. God's presence continued with him and once again he gained favor as his integrity, character, and skill were recognized.

Wherever Joseph went, he grew in favor, character and skill, and he never stopped believing God's dream for him. He kept God's dream tucked deep inside his heart. He had the gift of dream interpretation, and accurately interpreted the dreams of two of Pharaoh's servants, who had been placed in prison temporarily. The cupbearer would be restored to his position; the baker would be hanged. He asked the cupbearer to remember him when he was restored. He was forgotten. He wasn't bitter, believing "God had forgotten him", nor did he turn his back on God because he was "abandoned and things were going from bad to worse." He believed God and continued to grow in whatever soil God placed him in. Two years went by and finally Joseph had his "suddenly".

Because Joseph had lived an excellent life and was known for using his gift of dream interpretation with accuracy, he was cleaned and brought before Pharaoh to interpret a dream that deeply troubled him. Pharaoh's wisemen could not help him, but God wanted to through Joseph. Joseph accurately interpreted the symbolism of the dreams and explained to Pharaoh God's warning through his dream. There would be seven years of great wealth and prosperity followed by seven years of want and famine. Pharaoh recognized the hand of God on Joseph and rewarded him by making him overseer of the lands of Egypt. During the years of plenty, Joseph gathered the harvest and prepared for the years of famine. When famine struck, Joseph's brothers came in search of provisions. They did not recognize him because he had matured and no longer resembled a Hebrew. He was now an Egyptian. They were sent away and ordered to return with Joseph's younger brother Benjamin.

Upon their return, he revealed his identity. They suffered great remorse for what they had done, but nonetheless, Joseph forgave them. There was a beautiful reunion as Joseph was united with his father. God not only restored the relationships and healed the heart of a grieving father, but due to Joseph's high position, he was able to preserve an entire nation from starvation. What man meant for evil, God used for good. Joseph followed God, kept his heart from bitterness, grew in wisdom, skill, character, and favor, and worked toward the dream in his heart. God taught him to dream bigger and used every detail of Joseph's journey to prepare him for greatness. God knew the kind of man needed for the position he had planned for him. He knew the kind of character and experience he would need. Instead of seeing a pit, a prison, a false accusation, or slavery, Joseph kept his eyes on God. He knew God's heart and trusted that God had his. Even when tempted to despair, feeling forgotten in prison, Joseph had to have realized that man does not promote you; God does. He knew if he had self-promotion in his heart, he would not be able to stand in front of Pharaoh. As it was, Joseph served the person in front of him with his gift. It made no difference if it was a servant in a prison or the Pharaoh on the throne. Joseph had been humbled by his journey and he allowed the tests in his life to promote him, rather than destroy him. God uses everything. He wants our trust, so He can broaden our shoulders and teach us how to dream bigger. Joseph stepped out of the boat, so to speak, and kept his eyes on his God.

"...man does not promote you...God does."

Our Own Joseph Journey

We ended up taking the call to come back to New Jersey so Troy could be a family pastor back in October 2015: our "curveball." Our position seemed to have nothing to do with the end vision God gave us back in Oregon, but it was part of the process. It has been a place of healing and preparation for the vision. God has brought so much healing and understanding to us during our time here. We have had a good life and are surrounded by amazing and powerful people, all hungry for more. This journey that we thought would be over in a few months has taken us ten years now. We have come full circle. How did we stay sane and not break, even though the journey has taken longer than we thought? We said yes to God, and we don't need to understand everything. He is faithful and He does not lie. We will eventually step into the full vision that God gave us years ago, because we are speaking God's truth over our lives and "*calling those things which do not exist as though they did*" (Romans 4:17). Joseph was given a dream and then thrown in a pit, sold as a slave, promoted and yet still not free, falsely accused and imprisoned, but then raised up to a position of great authority. We too, like Joseph, have grown in character, died to self and our own understanding, gained skills along the journey, and positioned ourselves to not be tempted by the world. We say yes to God before He even asks. We have learned to be content in all situations, because our lives are not our own. Do we sometimes slip and walk outside of rest? Yes. But we have learned to quickly repent and enter back in.

We have a history with God now. We don't understand it all. We still have questions that have not been answered. He is faithful and He keeps His promises. Our yes is His amen. We have all of heaven at our back. If you had told me at the beginning of our journey what would be required of me, I may have said no. But now, I wouldn't change a thing, because I have learned that He is the Promised Land. He is the destination. And I am a loved daughter of the King of kings. It's not about us anyway. It's all about Him and establishing His Kingdom on earth.

When you have overcome the obstacles discussed in the previous pages, all of you will be ready to encounter all of Him. If there are areas not glistening with hope in your life, remember that is evidence of a stronghold and an area where you are choosing to live in mediocrity. When God puts His finger on those areas not glistening with hope, it is an invitation to allow the Holy Spirit to ask you some digging questions. This is so you can find the root, break partnership with it, exchange it for His truth, and step out in freedom. With the obstacles removed, you can take on any mountain, attain any vision, believe for any promise, and be that glorious bride. With the keys in your possession, you will learn how to sustain your freedom, and not fade away as so many shooting stars do. Humility is key.

The Place of Greatest Testing

Many people are blinded by achievement or relax when they have finally entered their "Promised Land", thinking their reward is God's approval. Surprisingly, this is actually the place of greatest testing. Proverbs 27:21 in the Passion Translation states; *"Fire is the way to test the purity of silver and gold, but the character of a man is tested by giving him a measure of fame."* Andrew Wommack, in *Financial Stewardship*, states, **"Real prosperity is defined by how much you give away, not by how much we keep for ourselves."** We are channels of God's goodness to the world. Provision flows through us to others in the same way a distributary stream flows from a larger source of water out into the reach of those away from the source. A prosperous soul reflects the generous heart of the Father and knows his Source is never ending. He enjoys the benefits of his position as resources flow through him, but his ultimate goal is not to collect the fullest reservoir, but rather be a channel of those resources to others. Although prosperity has a lot to do with money, I would be remiss to not point out that prosperity can also be wisdom, love and respect, honor, influence, position, success, possessions, gifts and talents, etc. You get the picture. Whatever prosperity you have been endowed with, it is meant to be given away and shared as more flows into you. The ultimate goal for Kingdom wealth is not just having money, influence, etc. work for you, but going one step further and having these resources working for the Kingdom. The only way to sustain success is to stay humble in the fear of the Lord, keep on the path of wisdom, and never forget that God is the source of your prosperity. When you rely on your prosperity or success, instead of recognizing God as your Source, that is idolatry. You will need God more than ever in the palaces of life, those places of prosperity. God gives a clear charge to those who have stepped into abundance. 1 Timothy 6:17-19 states,

> *Command those who are rich in this present age not to be haughty, nor to trust in uncertain riches but in the living God, who gives us richly all things to enjoy. Let them do good, that they be rich in good works, ready to give, willing to share, storing up for themselves a good foundation for the time to come, that they may lay hold on eternal life.*

I love what Pastor Jim Baker says about the abundant life (p134),

> *The abundant life that Jesus came to bring is not so you can get rich, but so you can develop a prosperous soul and can live from the resources of the Kingdom in every situation. In doing this, you never meet a situation in your own strength, but in the strength of Christ.*

We can never grow too big for our own britches. He is the destination. He is the Promised Land. He brings you out of Egypt to Himself.

"He is the destination.
He is the Promised Land.
He brings you out of Egypt to Himself."

Define Your Destination

Our total vision hasn't been fulfilled yet. We are taking it in pieces and investing in renewing our mindsets so that we will be able to carry the vision. We have entered our Promised Land though. We started this journey focused on the wrong destination, which led us to disillusionment with the process. We were given a vision and the goal was to get there. It was almost as one would have a goal to become a doctor with the educational path laid out before them, one step at a time. Kingdom is not like that. If He is not the destination, then everything else will be skewed. God needed to teach us how to unpack a vision and tap into the heart motives of what makes us truly come alive.

I have always had a spirit of excellence. I have always had expensive taste and loved beautiful things. We were designed for greatness. As I said previously, I have big dreams and a generous heart but pushed that all down thinking that I must be materialistic, selfish, or had a misplaced love of money. These self-condemning thoughts seemed contrary to anything else in my life, but nevertheless, I believed them, keeping my dreams capped and submitted to religious "beliefs." I had grown up believing that money was evil. The truth is, the "love" of money is the root of all evil (1 Timothy 6:10). I love how Matthew 6:24 puts it in the Passion Translation,

"How could you worship two gods at the same time? You will have to hate one and love the other, or be devoted to one and despise the other. You can't worship the true God while enslaved to the god of money." God wants us to prosper but, like in the area of food, He doesn't want anything to control our hearts or affections. He doesn't want anything to enslave us. He is our Provider. He will give us the provision for the vision. We are not to pursue money, but rather we will attract money when our hearts are in the right place and we have the mind of Christ in regards to stewardship.

Getting to the Heart of the Matter

I did an exercise in Jim Baker's Wealth with God course that did just that. Because we were learning about how God viewed money and prosperity, I was learning how to exchange my poverty mindset about money and God's purpose for wealth, with the truth from God's Word. Pastor Jim asked, "Who desires more money?" Very few raised their hands because they didn't think it was proper to want money. He challenged us to not think of desiring money as selfish. Desiring money is selfish when you only think about the needs of you and your household, not taking into account the needs of others around you. I was challenged to first believe it was okay to be wealthy, and second, to ask myself why I wanted wealth. It's okay to ask this question, you know. Remember, I am not talking about pursuing wealth (wealth is not the goal). I am addressing the fact that it is okay to possess wealth, so long as it does not possess you. He is our source. Big difference. Allow the Holy Spirit access to the depths of your heart. He wants to do heart surgery on some of you. Money is the kindergarten level in the Kingdom. I know this is not a book on finances, but we are addressing stepping into your God-sized vision and usually God-sized visions require financing. We need to have our money issues settled, so that we can do the greater things in the Kingdom.

"...it is okay to possess wealth, so long as it does not possess you."

Wisdom has taught me that money is a tool. A much-needed tool, if one wants to build the Kingdom, yes? To build a house you need a hammer and nails. To build a kingdom, you need money. How silly we are to think a hammer and nails are essential for the job, but view money as a necessary evil. They are both tools. As I began to ask myself why I wanted to be wealthy, it allowed the Holy Spirit access to the deep motives of my heart and ultimately the desires placed there by God in the first place. My first answer to why I want to be wealthy was because I wanted to get out of the box of limitations over my life and break free of that constant feeling that there was not enough. Money, or lack of it, defined every decision I made.

The second question, "Why don't you want to be limited?" probed further. My answer; "I can't express what is truly in my heart. I have big dreams and a big vision, but nothing to back it up. I can't build what is in my heart." The third question continued, "Why is it important to express what is in your heart?" My answer finally hit the chord. I want people around me to know how loved they are. That's when the tears flowed, because I realized the truth that broke the "materialistic" lie. It all came down to love. I had grown up "feeling" invisible, living off the crumbs, and unsupported. God wanted to heal that broken part of my heart, so that I could reveal His heart to others. I did not know Him as Provider. I had grown up feeling that it was all up to me to make things happen, unaware I had a Father in Heaven who had unlimited resources to back up the dreams He had placed in my heart. This exercise revealed to me that I have His extravagant heart, with His extravagant backing. He has a love without limits. Here the enemy had come against my destiny all my life, wanting me to believe I was greedy and materialistic. But the truth is, I want to spend my life demonstrating to people around me the extravagant love of my heavenly Father…without limits.

This is the heart of our vision. God has a unique vision custom tailored to each individual, and once you get clear with that vision, and clarify that it is indeed from God, then believe He will give you the provision for that vision. Get curious about what motivates your heart and ask those deep, penetrating heart questions so that you can truly step out into your destiny. That is what most people miss when they don't probe the depths, and ask the why questions that get to the roots. My vision is to create a wealthy and prosperous life in spirit, body, and soul; and remove the limitations preventing me from fulfilling my mission, so I can spend my life demonstrating to people the extravagant love of the Father. Troy's vision is similar and it is why we make a great team. His heart is to influence people to become all that they were created to be, so they can live effective and fulfilling lives in the Kingdom. I would encourage you to get to the root of your heart mission. For it is from there that all your decisions will flow. Make sure that the root is grounded in intimacy with the Father, for His heart truly is the destination.

"I want to spend my life demonstrating to people around me the extravagant love of my heavenly Father… without limits."

A Misplaced Motivation

People who unknowingly misplace their heart on any other destination arrive with the big question, "What now?" They end up disappointed, somewhat lost, and unfulfilled. Take the very potent contrast between Harold Abrahams and Eric Liddell in the movie *Chariots of Fire*. Eric ran because he loved running. Eric states, **"I believe God made me for a purpose, but He also made me fast. And when I run, I feel His pleasure."** When he won the 400-meter gold medal in the 1920 Olympics he was pleased, but his focus was on his relationship with God. He returned to China to continue his family's missionary work, which is where his heart's passion truly rested. In contrast, Abrahams's motivation for winning and his destination was fueled by his previous losses and the rivalry he had with his two older brothers. He had something to prove.

In the movie, he makes the point that he was more afraid of winning than losing because his focus in life had all been for this one moment and now it was defining him. He confesses, "In one hour's time I will be out there again. I will raise my eyes and look down that corridor; 4 feet wide, with 10 lonely seconds to justify my whole existence. But will I?" He continues later, "I have known the fear of losing, but now I am almost too frightened to win." In the depths of the wilderness time, when we would cry out to God for direction and provision, the only answer we would receive was, "I love you," or "Pursue Me." It was the most frustrating, and seemingly cruel answer, because we were still learning how to steward a vision through intimacy with the Father and we didn't understand that the key was in His answer...Himself.

We were desperately wanting to know and do His will and couldn't understand why He wouldn't answer us. On this side, we realize He was. He was answering us in exactly the way we needed to hear. The answer was to know how loved we were. The answer was to pursue Him. I love how Pastor Jim Baker puts it in *How Heaven Invades Your Finances* (p.25),

> *Regardless of what God is truly like, you are unlikely to experience God any greater than your concept of Him...God is who He is regardless of what you think. But your experience of God will be based on who you think God is and how He deals with us...Your impression of God will determine what you experience from God.*

He knew we had a whole lot of unlearning still to do. We were still operating with God in a box and He wanted out. Until we understood what it meant for Him to be the destination, we would forever be wandering in the wilderness.

40 Years or 40 Days?

This is how I know it is possible to eliminate years off of your wilderness time. There is no need to wander in the wilderness for 40 years in unbelief. Jesus understood who He was and who His Father was and His purpose was clear: to do the Fathers will. This made all the difference. His 40-day wilderness experience was a time to face down the enemy and model for us the importance of identity and living from the Spirit versus the flesh. He was anything but mediocre. He modeled for us a life on the water and He is calling us out there with Him. In a world that tells you to keep it safe and live for comfort, I want to send out a new message: step out of the boat and walk on water. Church, wake up! Ask God for a vision so big you can't do it on your own. Call out to God like Peter called out to Him, "Lord, if it is You, command me to come to You on the water." Initiate stepping out of the boat, because He is there waiting for you and bids you, "Come." Whether that be taking a leap of faith and stepping out into a dream you have allowed fear to squelch, or taking a risk and praying for someone's healing. Maybe it is your own healing you are contending for. Take it. Don't let the enemy talk you out of it. You don't need any more faith. You have it all inside of you. Let it manifest through your belief. You will have what you believe for. Believe what God says and speak it out over your life. Come into agreement with your true identity and the plans for your life.

"Come."

Be A Water Walker

If you need help on this journey and how to navigate the waters, receive counsel from others walking on the water, not those still in the boat. If you want to learn how to slay a giant, hang out with giant slayers…if you want to walk on water, hang out with Water Walkers. We are available to lead and mentor you into the deeper life, the Kingdom life, through online courses, classes, personal coaching, training, and through other resources. You can find us on the web at **www.IAmAWaterWalker.com**. If others have gone before you and thrown you a rope, take it and spare yourself the pain of some of the trial and error. Mistakes and pain do not have to be your teachers. Let Holy Spirit guide you and surround yourself with other Kingdom believers hungry for the deeper life. Don't dream with the devil. Instead dream with God and step out of the boat and feel the sensation of the water under your feet as you walk toward your Promised Land…your beautiful Bridegroom. Rock the boat and then jump out and start living the life you were created to live. You have a destiny awaiting you. You have a legacy to leave for others to follow. What are you waiting for? Be a Water Walker!

"…if you want to walk on water, hang out with Water Walkers."

You'll never reach your destiny unless you step out of the boat.

You Are Just One Step Away…

Secret #24

With the Spirits leading, don't be afraid to pursue issues or topics that cause contention. Most likely the enemy is guarding a secret to your breakthrough and he doesn't want to lose ground when you are awakened to the deeper things of God.

Don't be more afraid of the enemy deceiving you than you are trusting God to lead you.

Secret #25

You can have what you believe for, so start believing what you have.

Secret #26

The journey equips you with a bigger vision, a wider sphere of influence, stronger character, more skills, a humble heart, and the capacity to hold what God has called and equipped you to carry. So, embrace the journey in the fear of the Lord.

Secret #27

Any area not glistening with hope reveals a lie you are believing and results in an unconscious choice of living in mediocrity in that area.

Go after it, break partnership with it, and exchange it for the abundance offered to you through the Cross and Resurrection of Jesus.

Secret #28

God brings you out of Egypt to Himself.

He is the destination.

References

Scripture taken from the New King James Version®. Copyright © 1982 by Thomas Nelson. Used by permission. All rights reserved.

Scripture quotations marked TPT are from The Passion Translation®. Copyright © 2017, 2018 by Passion & Fire Ministries, Inc. Used by permission. All rights reserved. ThePassionTranslation.com.

The Invitation

1. I heard Sean speak on *100X's, The 31 Days of Wisdom Challenge*, Day 16 on Facebook January 2020. He coauthored a book, *YouTube Secrets: The Ultimate Guide to Growing Your Following and Making Money* as a Video Influencer by Sean Cannell and Benji Travis.

2. The Man in the Arena is a quote from a speech entitled *"Citizenship in a Republic"* given by former President of the United States, Theodore Roosevelt. This was taken from a passage of that 35-page speech, found on page 7.

3. The rock-climbing analogy was adapted from a book called *Habitudes: Images That Form Leadership Habits & Attitudes: For Self Leadership: The Art of Leading Yourself* by Dr. Tim Elmore. His book series on leadership habits and attitudes is fantastic. I have taken my older children through the training and found it very inspiring and practical.

Chapter One

1. Dr. Brené Brown, www.brenebrown.com, author of *Daring Greatly: How the courage to Be Vulnerable Transforms the Way We Live, Love, Parent, and Lead* and many other great books. Her TED Talk on The Power of Vulnerability has been viewed over 41 million times. She is amazing and so inspiring.

Chapter Two

1. Author John Eldredge wrote the book, *Wild at Heart, Discovering the Secret of a Man's Soul*. I read the quote referenced in his book and have treasured it in my heart, although he was quoting Second Century Saint, Saint Irenaeus.

2. I have learned so much from Pastor Jim Baker, senior pastor of Zion Christian Fellowship in Powell Ohio. He has a fantastic online course called *Wealth with God Masterclass*, which can be found online at www.wealthwithgod.com. I highly recommend everyone work through this life-changing course. He also has a powerful book titled, *How Heaven Invades Your Finances Book 1 Building the Foundation for Supernatural Finances*. It is available on Amazon.com. I have used all quotes with permission.

Chapter Three

1. Pastor Paul Martini, Associate Pastor at Life Center in Harrisburg, PA, (www.MartiniMinistry.com), all quotes and references used with permission.

Chapter Four

1. Charles Capps, *God's Creative Power (www.cappsministries.com)*. His little books are powerful and small enough to read in a sitting. He is all about the power of our words.

Chapter Five

1. *Love After Marriage: A Journey into Deeper Spiritual, Emotional, and Sexual Oneness* (book) by Lori and Barry Burns, www.nothinghidden.com. They offer books, courses, and events where they teach tools to couples as well as singles on deeper intimacy. I referenced one of their tools, the "1,2,3, Skidoo tool", we learned from them when we hosted an event at our church. I highly recommend their book as it teaches you how to invite Holy Spirit into your marriage relationship. Used with permission.

2. Pastor Paul Martini, Associate Pastor at Life Center in Harrisburg, PA, (www.MartiniMinistry.com), He came to speak at a conference at our church. I used all quotes and references with permission.

3. Francis Frangipanae, *The Three Battlegrounds*, p43.

Chapter Six

1. Graham Cooke, author, speaker, www.brilliantperspectives.com. I subscribe to Graham's daily Brilliant Perspectives in my inbox every day. I am constantly pausing the video so I can take notes because literally everything he says is brilliant.

2. Movie, *An Interview with God* starring David Strathairn, 2018, available for purchase on Amazon.com.

Chapter Seven

1. *The Life-Changing Magic of Tidying Up: The Japanese Art of Decluttering and Organizing* by Marie Kondo is a fantastic book that revolutionized my home and thinking about possessions as well as the past and why we hold onto things.

Chapter Eight

1. Doug Addison, Los Angeles, California, InLight Connection, "A Strategic Season to Hear God More Clearly" as posted on Elijah List April 29, 2020.

2. Dr. Scott Stoll, MD www.drscottstoll.com. His book *Alive* is available on Amazon.com. I am blessed to call the Stoll family amongst our dearest and most intimate of friends. They don't just talk the talk, but they live the walk. Dr. Stoll is a Spirit-filled believer and one of the most researched physicians I have ever met. His book and their lives have been a beautiful model of God's healing perspective of food while keeping food in its proper place: nourishing and sustaining the body so we can in turn live the "abundant life." Food can still be totally delightful, but it doesn't have to control you.

3. Pastor Jim Baker, senior pastor of Zion Christian Fellowship in Powell, Ohio. His book *How Heaven Invades Your Finances Book 1 Building the Foundation for Supernatural Finances* is available on Amazon.com. All quotes used with permission.

4. William Wood: Preacher, Healing Evangelist, Exhorter, and Founder of Relentless (www.globalawakening.com); all quotes and references used with permission.

5. Bill Johnson, Senior Leader at Bethel Church in Redding California, author of *When Heaven Invades Earth, Hosting the Presence: Unveiling Heaven's Agenda, Face to Face with God: Get Ready for a Life-Changing Encounter with God*, and more. He is one of my favorite Bible teachers.

6. Jaime Cross, CEO & Founder of MIG & the Her Effect®, (www.migsoap.com) and (www.thehereffect.com). Can I just tell you how much I love this woman, her products, and her mission? She is such an inspiration. Definitely check her out! All quotes used with permission.

7. Steve and Wendy Backlund, Igniting Hope Ministries (www.ignitinghope.com) - Steve and Wendy have a powerful ministry of mind transformation through declarations. Their conference, *Abounding Hope and Joy Conference* is so life changing. I have listened to it several times. I have also read several of their books, amongst my favorites are *Victorious Mindsets, Let's Just Laugh at That, Victorious Emotions*, and *Possessing Joy*.

Chapter Ten

1. *The Wizard of Oz*, produced by Metro-Goldwyn-Mayer, 1939.

2. Pastor Jim Baker, senior pastor of Zion Christian Fellowship in Powell Ohio. He has a life-changing online course called *Wealth with God Masterclass*, which can be found online at www.wealthwithgod.com. I highly recommend everyone work through this amazing course. All quotes used with permission.

3. *Chariots of Fire*, 1981.

28 Secrets to Becoming a Water Walker

In the book I have interchanged secrets and keys in referring to these truths because there are secrets that need to be discovered to walk on water, which are ultimately the keys to open the doors to your destiny.

Secret #1: Determine to step out of the boat.

Secret #2: Faith is living in expectancy, and not in expectation.

Secret #3: When we sow financial seeds, we demonstrate our faith and intimacy level in a Father who is a never-ending source of provision.

Secret #4: Don't go this journey alone. But don't take counsel from someone you wouldn't trade places with either.

Secret #5: Learn to love the process.

Secret #6: Fear is dreaming with the devil. Know the Word of God so you can recognize the lies of the enemy.

Secret #7: Don't let your experiences, disappointments or disillusions form your theology. Rather let the Word of God renew your mind with truth. God's Word trumps our experiences.

Secret #8: Build your house – Proverbs 24:3-4.

Secret #9: Know God and know your identity.

Secret #10: Rest is your greatest warfare.

Secret #11: Laughter is good medicine, so laugh at the enemy.

Secret #12: Free will was God's idea. Separate the man-made god of religion and get to know the God of the Bible.

Secret #13: God is good.

Secret #14: Eat from the Tree of Life, not from the Tree of the Knowledge of Good and Evil.

Secret #15: The past does not define you…God does.

Secret #16: Clarify in your life what is a belief versus a mental agreement.

Secret #17: Learn to hear God's voice. Get alone and quiet with God until all the other voices have faded, and it is only His voice you hear.

Secret #18: Fast the flesh. Soak. Pray in the Spirit. Worship. Journal. Declare. Repeat.

Secret #19: We fight from victory, not for it.

Secret #20: Grow up and walk with Wisdom.

Secret # 21: Money is an intimacy issue. What you believe about wealth, money, and prosperity is essential to walking in a Kingdom mindset.

Secret #22: See yourself as God sees you, His radiant bride.

Secret #23: Treat the Scripture as your inheritance and treasure every word.

Secret #24: With the Spirit's leading, don't be afraid to pursue issues or topics that cause contention. Most likely the enemy is guarding a secret to your breakthrough and he doesn't want to lose ground when you are awakened to the deeper things of God. Don't be more afraid of the enemy deceiving you than you are trusting God to lead you.

Secret #25: You can have what you believe for so start believing what you have.

Secret #26: The journey equips you with a bigger vision, a wider sphere of influence, stronger character, more skills, a humble heart, and the capacity to hold what God has called and equipped you to carry. Embrace the journey in the fear of the Lord.

Secret #27: Any area not glistening with hope reveals a lie you are believing and results in an unconscious choice of living in mediocrity in that area. Go after it, break partnership with it, and exchange it for the abundance offered to you through the Cross and Resurrection of Jesus.

Secret #28: God brings you out of Egypt to Himself. He is the destination.

APPENDIX TWO

Inheritance Confessions

———✦———

Guard what you think because it will become your words. Guard what
you say because it will become what you do. Guard what you do
because it will become your character. Declarations are an invitation to
renew one's mind in order to speak life. You must first renew your mind
with the goodness of God.

~Ahab Alhindi, Limitless Intimacy

ROMANS 4:17B: "GOD, WHO GIVES LIFE TO THE DEAD AND CALLS THOSE
THINGS WHICH DO NOT EXIST AS THOUGH THEY DID…"

This is just a sample and a way to get started confessing the Word of God over yourself until your mind is renewed with the truth. We demolish strongholds in our lives through declaring the truth (2 Corinthians 10:4-5). We overcome each obstacle by confessing the truth in its place. We don't come to God pleading with Him; we come agreeing with what He has already finished. By renewing our minds, we are trading the images in our head for images of truth. We are not denying the facts, which exist, we simply confess the truth of God's Word and establish His unseen and desired reality. We come into alignment with God's truth, thinking, and speaking like Him. For example, when we see lack, we know through the study of God's Word, it is not His nature or His plan. We simply call forth provision and abundance and align ourselves to His ways of receiving provision and abundance.

I wrote these confessions as a prescription to pray when you have lost sight of the truth, but I would encourage you to pray them every day so that you don't lose sight in the first place. Meditate in His Word day and night and you will be like a tree firmly planted by streams of water, which yield its fruit in its season. Your leaf will not whither and whatever you do will prosper (Psalm 1: 2-3). When the image you have inside is truth, there will be no convincing you otherwise.

When I feel afraid, I confess:

God you have not given me a spirit of fear, but of love, power, and a sound mind. My mind has been made perfect in your love and perfect love casts out all fear. When I am afraid, I just have to be reminded that greater are You who lives inside of me than he that is in the world. I sit enthroned under the shadow of Shaddai. I am hidden in the strength of God Most High. God, You are the hope that holds me, and the Stronghold to shelter me, the only God for me, and my great confidence. You rescue me from every hidden trap of the enemy, and protect me from false accusation and any deadly curse. Your massive arms are wrapped around me, protecting me. I can run under Your covering of majesty and hide, for Your arms of faithfulness are a shield keeping me from harm. I never need worry about an attack of demonic forces at night nor have to fear a spirit of darkness coming against me. I don't fear a thing! Whether by night or by day, demonic danger will not trouble me nor will the powers of evil that have been launched against me.

Even in a time of disaster, with thousands and thousands being killed, I will remain unscathed and unharmed. I will be a spectator as the wicked perish in judgment, for they will be paid back for what they have done! Because I live my life within the shadow of God Most High, my secret hiding place, I will always be shielded from harm. How then could evil prevail against me or disease infect me? God sends angels with special orders to protect me wherever I go, defending me from all harm. If I walk into a trap, my angels will be there for me and keep me from stumbling. I will even walk unharmed among the fiercest powers of darkness, trampling every one of them beneath my feet! For the Lord has told me that because I have delighted in Him as my great lover, He will greatly protect me. He will set me in a high place, safe and secure before His face. He will answer my cry for help every time I pray, and I will find and feel His presence even in my time of pressure and trouble. He will be my glorious hero and give me a feast. I will be satisfied with a full life and with all that He does for me. For I will enjoy the fullness of my salvation in God! (2 Timothy 1:7, 1 John 4:18, 2 Kings 6, Psalm 91 TPT)

Psalm 18 is another great one to personalize. It reveals the character and love of God for His beloved. The image will forever stay in your heart when you are afraid and you will not be shaken.

When I fear lack of provision I confess:

The Lord is my Shepherd and I shall not be in want. My God supplies all my needs according to His riches in glory through Christ Jesus. I have sown bountifully and therefore I will reap bountifully into my bosom: good measure, pressed down, shaken together, and running over. So, in the same measure that I give, it will be measured back to me. I am a cheerful giver and You make all grace abound toward me that I always, having all sufficiency in all things, may have an abundance for every good work. God, you want my finances to grow to the point that any time there is a financial need that comes across my path, and I am led to give, I will have an abundant stream to meet that need that flows from the vaults of heaven. I am a funnel from heaven to earth.

I do not serve or follow other gods. I worship God alone and will not forget Him. Therefore, He gives me the power to get wealth in keeping with His covenant with Abraham. You take pleasure in seeing your children prosper. I will not walk in debt. I will have more than enough to fulfill the dreams and assignments given to me to walk in and enough left over to help others walk in and fulfill their destinies as well. I have provision for the vision! I delight myself in You, therefore you give me the desires of my heart. You have come that I might have life and have it more abundantly. My cup is not just full, it is overflowing. Christ has redeemed me from the curse of the law and He has redeemed me and my household from poverty, sickness, and lack. I am blessed in my body, in my possessions, and in the land that I steward. It will always produce a good harvest. I am blessed in the city and blessed in the country. My enemies will scatter. My table will always have plenty and I will be blessed when I go in and come out.

The Lord will bless my storehouses and everything that I lay my hand to. He will bless me in the land He will give me and always provide rain in its season. He gives me all the financial means I need to accomplish His Kingdom purposes through me. I have a generous heart and the more money I have, the more impact I can make, so bless me Lord, financially. The Lord will establish me and set me apart. I will be a lender and not a borrower. I am the head and not the tail. Because I fear the Lord and walk in His ways, I will be happy and eat from the labor of my hands. It will go well with me all the days of my life as my family walks in fruitfulness and abundance. I will live a long, good life and see my children's children. You are a good Father and you want to see your children prospering and reigning in life. (Psalm 23, Philippians 4:19, 2Corinthians 9:6-8, Luke 6:38, Deuteronomy 8:18-19, Galatians 3:13-14, Psalm 35:27, John 10:10, Psalm 37:4, Deuteronomy 28, Psalm 128)

When I have lost faith and forgotten who I am, I confess:

I speak life and no corrupt word comes from my mouth, but only that which will edify and impart grace to those who hear. Life is in the power of my tongue. I have been delivered from the powers of darkness and placed in the Kingdom of God's dear Son. I am born of God and have faith that has overcome the world living on the inside of me. For greater is He who is inside of me than he who is in the world. I can do all things through Christ who strengthens me. I am a new creation in Christ. The old has gone. Behold, all things are made new. I am the righteousness of God because Jesus became sin in my place. I speak life and no corrupt word comes from my mouth, but only that which is good and necessary edification, that it may impart grace to the hearers. I am of a chosen race, a royal priesthood, a holy nation; God's own people. He has called me out of darkness into His marvelous light. I am born again therefore I see the Kingdom of God. He brought me out into a broad place and saved me because He delights in me. Because I am in Christ, You have crowned me with glory and honor and set me over the works of Your hands. You have put all things under my feet. No man shall take me out of Your hand, for I have eternal life. I am a child of God. Jesus gave me the keys to the Kingdom and I have authority to use His name. That which I bind on earth is bound in heaven. That which I loose on earth is loosed in heaven. I wear the full armor of God: the belt of truth, the breastplate of righteousness, the shoes of the gospel of peace, the shield of faith, the helmet of salvation, and the sword of the Spirit. I do battle in the heavenlies from a place of victory not for it, and I take down those principalities, powers, rulers of darkness, and spiritual hosts of wickedness and render them ineffective against me in the name of Jesus. I am complete in Him who is the head of all principality and power. For I am His workmanship, created in Christ Jesus for good works, which God prepared beforehand that I should walk in them. (Colossians 1:13, 1 John 5:4-5, 1 John 4:4, Philippians 4:13, 2 Corinthians 5:17, Proverbs 18:21, 1 Peter 2:9, John 3:3, Psalm 18:19, Hebrews 2, Ephesians 4:29, 2 Corinthians 5:21, John 10:28-29, John 1:12-13, Matthew 16:19, Ephesians 6:12-17, Colossians 2:10, Ephesians 2:10)

When I find myself struggling with an old mindset I confess:

I will not let the Word of God depart from before my eyes because it is life to me and healing to my flesh. I am a believer and these signs do follow me: In the name of Jesus I cast out demons, I speak with new tongues, I lay hands on the sick and they do recover. My household and I will serve the Lord. I want to be His disciple and therefore I deny myself, take up my cross, and follow Him by my own free will. I plan my course, but the Lord establishes my steps. I walk by the Spirit and do not gratify the desires of the flesh. I choose to eat from the Tree of Life and not from the Tree of the Knowledge of Good and Evil. I have a new heart and a new spirit. I have the mind of Christ. I do not conform to the patterns of this world, but am transformed by the renewing of my mind. (Proverbs 4:21-22, Mark 16:17-18, Joshua 24:15, Proverbs 16:9, Galatians 5: 16-17, Genesis 2:16-17, Ezekiel 18:30-32, Philippians 2:5, Romans 12:2)

When I am having difficulty overcoming the past, focusing on the present or fearing the future I confess:

I have the mind of Christ. I have been crucified with Christ and no longer live, but Christ lives in me. Anything attached to my old nature is nailed to the cross and I walk in resurrection life now. I am a new creature in Christ. The old is gone and behold all things have been made new. He knows the plans He has for me. They are plans to prosper me and not harm me. He gives me a hope and a future. God laughs at my enemies because He knows their end, therefore, I too laugh at my enemies for they speak contrary to who I am in Christ. When the enemy reminds me of my past, I remind him of his future. I have the Spirit of truth dwelling inside of me, who will guide me into all truth and tell me of the things to come. Therefore, I confess I have perfect knowledge in every situation and in all the circumstances of my life. For I have the wisdom of God and the mind of Christ. I trust in the Lord and lean not on my own understanding. In all my ways I acknowledge Him and He directs my path. The Lord will perfect that which concerns me. Because the Word of God dwells in me richly, I walk in wisdom. I am filled with the knowledge of the Lord's will in all wisdom and spiritual understanding. (Philippians 4:11-13, John 10:10, Romans 8:28, Psalm 2:4, Philippians 1:6, Galatians 2:20, 2 Corinthians 5:17, Colossians 1:27, Jeremiah 29:11, Revelation 20:10, John 16:13, James

1:5, Proverbs 3:5-6, Psalm 138:8, Matthew 16:24, Colossians 3:16, Colossians 1:9)

When I struggle with giving in to an old, dead nature by walking in pride, ungratefulness, greed, addiction, jealousy, selfishness, etc. I confess:

I have the mind of Christ. I have been crucified with Christ and no longer live, but Christ lives in me. Anything attached to my old nature is nailed to the cross and I walk in resurrection life now. I am a new creature in Christ. The old is gone and behold all things have been made new. I am not angry, selfish, greedy, or prideful because those things do not exist in Christ. They are dead and I am alive in Him. I put off the old man and put on the new man. When I was a child I thought and acted as a child, but now I am a new man and have put childish ways away from me. I am an imitator of God because I am dearly loved by God. I live in love and give myself in love just as Christ gave Himself in love. I am kind, compassionate, and forgiving just as Christ forgave me. I am generous because the Lord became poor so that through His poverty, I could become rich. I give thanks in all things for the Lord is good and is worthy of my gratitude. I can do all things through Christ who gives me strength. (Philippians 2:5-8, Galatians 2:20, 1 Corinthians 2:16, 2 Corinthians 5:17, Ephesians 4:14-32, 1 Corinthians 13:11, Ephesians5:1-2, Ephesians 4:32, 2 Corinthians 8:1-9, Psalm 100, 1 Thessalonian 5:18, Philippians 4:13)

Get to Know Rebecca

My Tribe

Troy, the man of my dreams and my rock, is a relentless pursuer of the deeper life. Smart is the new sexy. He is a homestead chicken expert and all-around funny guy. His self-claim to fame is being the more logical one of us two (no comment). We have six amazing children, our "Brady Bunch" (3 girls and 3 boys). They are all artists in their own right with incredible destinies to pursue. They are my favorite people alive.

What I Would Do If I Were Not Busy Being Superwoman

If my house could clean itself, my children educate themselves, and my husband learn to cook more than pancakes, I would totally be an actress and in a role where I had to learn to sing and dance. I would love to be dressed in fabulous costumes and have people doing my hair and makeup all day. How fun to be paid to learn amazing things, in amazing places, with amazing people. Dream roles: Donna in *Mamma Mia*, Lizzy in *Pride and Prejudice*, Mia in *La La Land*, or Mary Crawley in *Downton Abbey*. An honorable mention (only because it was a male role) would, of course, be P.T. Barnum in *The Greatest Showman*. The opening scene with the music, "WOAH!", and the stomp of the feet on the bleachers...I literally hold my breath in excitement. I so want to do that scene...and I want the hat, jacket, and cane too. Truth be told…I actually think my greatest role is Superwoman, because although it feels at times that anyone can cook, clean, or educate my children, there is only one me for them, and I wouldn't want to miss a second of their lives. I will have to save my Ringmasters costume for another day. Right now, in my own circus, I wear a cape.

Things I Am Known For

Celebrations and making things fun and special, living intentionally, "organic" and "healthy", wisdom, a mother's heart, organization, Peace and Joy, Hygge, herbalism and making my own home remedies and body care products, a cozy and beautiful home in every season, taking pictures and creating picture albums, "Kondo ing"-I am not a saver, rocking out to 80's music with my thumb microphone and air guitar (sorry about the Footloose episode Ash - I hate it when I am so much cooler in my head than in real life), tea and biscotti, laughing too loud in a movie theatre, and being a wealth of information…(which is not the same as being a know-it-all.)

Things I'm NOT Known For

Saying anything in a few words (why use 10 words when you can use 1,000), chaos, small talk, processed or fast food, geography (that is a loaded subject), swimming in the "sharks' house", and using an outhouse. I just won't do it. Period.

Things That Light Me Up (there is so much…I think I am always pretty lit)

The presence of God and presents from God, my husband (especially when I catch him admiring me unexpectedly), "nuggle" times and dates with my

children, vision planning and dreaming with God, a clean house, that
"lightbulb" moment when people get a revelation of the extravagant love of
God and His amazing Kingdom and they exchange lies for the truth, funny
people, laughing!!!, traveling to beautiful places, tasting something so amazing
that it awakens the tear ducts and heaven invades earth as angels sing,
bouquets of herbal flowers from my garden in small white pitchers, farmers'
markets, firefly's in the summertime, glowing candles, a warm cozy fire,
pumpkins and apples in the fall, an afternoon to myself at home, feet pajamas
(on the children, not me), Christmastime, snow...especially the sound when
it falls, clean lavender scented sheets, a Jeep Wrangler with my favorite driving
playlist, the Blue Angels, camping—so long as I have my own toilet, my
favorite perfume, sassy earrings, cowgirl boots and heels, spa days, soup on
the stove, bread in the oven, and fun things scheduled on the calendar with
my best friends.

Favorites

Books: *Hidden Hand* by E.D.E.N. Southworth, *Nourished* by Lia Huber,
Redeeming Love by Francine Rivers, *Mandy* by Julie Andrews, the Bible
...duh, and all Chris Van Dusen books. (I love children's books.) I am an
avid reader, but am usually filling my time with books on Kingdom living,
marriage and parenting, DIY, cooking, or herbalism...rarely just a
pleasure read except when I have a child on my lap.

Movies: a movie has to have characters that move me and get inside my
head and heart, take me to a beautiful place or time, or else really make me
laugh or cry. So, if you are putting a gun to my head, and telling me I had

to choose, then *Little Women, About Time, The Chosen, Downton Abbey,* and *Sherlock Holmes BBC* are my top favs.

Favorite Songs/Artists: Sorry, no such thing. The list of music I don't like would be shorter. Music is just the soundtrack to life and there are different soundtracks for every activity. For instance: Chris Botti, Michael Bublé, Andrea Bocelli, Melody Gardot, or Diana Krall are perfect for cooking dinner. Scala and Kolacny or Libera are favorites in the fall and into Christmas, Bethel Worship I take with me on my walks, and we have already established my Lip-synch career to 80's music. Then, of course, there is the soundtrack that comes out when I am driving all by myself— yes, true freedom—that's the jeep soundtrack... but that is privileged information.

Favorite Foods: I love lots of fresh veggies and salads, sushi, spicy ethnic food, especially Thai and Indian, and I have a weakness for homemade hot fudge sundaes. I love my mom's cooking and eating at Kelli's.

Favorite Places: There is no place like home, but I love traveling to beautiful places, especially Maine. My bucket list is long. Watch out world … Here I come.

www.ingramcontent.com/pod-product-compliance
Lightning Source LLC
Chambersburg PA
CBHW051818090426
42736CB00011B/1535